GOVERNMENT PROCEDURES AND OPERATIONS

IRS AUDITS

SELECTION PROCESS AND CONTROLS FOR INDIVIDUALS, SMALL BUSINESS AND THE SELF-EMPLOYED

GOVERNMENT PROCEDURES AND OPERATIONS

Additional books in this series can be found on Nova's website under the Series tab.

Additional e-books in this series can be found on Nova's website under the eBooks tab.

GOVERNMENT PROCEDURES AND OPERATIONS

IRS AUDITS

SELECTION PROCESS AND CONTROLS FOR INDIVIDUALS, SMALL BUSINESS AND THE SELF-EMPLOYED

KARA BRADLEY
EDITOR

NOVINKA
New York

NOTICE TO THE READER

Library of Congress Cataloging-in-Publication Data

ISBN: 978-1-63485-724-6

Published by Nova Science Publishers, Inc. † New York

CONTENTS

PREFACE

Audit activities help ensure taxpayers pay the right amount of tax and help address the net $385 billion tax gap—the difference between the amount of taxes paid voluntarily and on time, and the amount owed. Audit programs in Internal Revenue Service's (IRS) Wage and Investment division (W&I) mainly cover refundable credits reported on the Form 1040, Individual Income Tax Return. The hundreds of thousands of taxpayers whom W&I interacts with annually during audits make it critical to apply the tax law fairly. Unfair selection would increase burden on taxpayers and reduce public confidence in IRS. This book reviews and describes the W&I process for selecting tax returns for audit, and determines how well W&I's audit selection procedures support its mission and goal to apply the tax law with integrity and fairness to all. This book also describes IRS's processes and controls for selecting Small Business/Self-Employed (SB/SE) taxpayers for audit; and determines how well SB/SE's selection processes and controls support its mission to apply the tax law with integrity and fairness to all.

In: IRS Audits
Editor: Kara Bradley

ISBN: 978-1-63485-724-6

Chapter 1

IRS Return Selection: Wage and Investment Division Should Define Audit Objectives and Refine Other Internal Controls*

United States Government Accountability Office

Why GAO Did This Study

Audit activities help ensure taxpayers pay the right amount of tax and help address the net $385 billion tax gap— the difference between the amount of taxes paid voluntarily and on time, and the amount owed. Audit programs in the Internal Revenue Service's (IRS) Wage and Investment division (W&I) mainly cover refundable credits reported on the Form 1040, Individual Income Tax Return. The hundreds of thousands of taxpayers whom W&I interacts with annually during audits make it critical to apply the tax law fairly. Unfair selection would increase burden on taxpayers and reduce public confidence in IRS.

GAO was asked to review W&I's audit selection process. This report (1) describes the W&I process for selecting tax returns for audit, and (2) determines how well W&I's audit selection procedures support its mission and goal to apply the tax law with integrity and fairness to all. GAO reviewed

* This is an edited, reformatted and augmented version of the United States Government Accountability Office publication, GAO-16-102, dated December 2015.

documentation on program procedures, an audit work plan, and various Internal Revenue Manual sections; analyzed audit data from fiscal years 2013 and 2014; and interviewed relevant IRS officials.

WHAT GAO RECOMMENDS

GAO recommends, among other things, that IRS establish program objectives and definitions of key terms such as "fairness" that apply to audit selection and use those definitions in assessing its selection performance; document selection processes more thoroughly; and document that changes to procedures are done in a timely manner. IRS generally agreed with all seven recommendations and provided additional comments reprinted in appendix II.

WHAT GAO FOUND

Three offices in the Internal Revenue Service's (IRS) Wage and Investment division (W&I) are responsible for selecting returns for audit. Most returns are selected via computer systems that automatically send notices to taxpayers based on certain criteria, such as the validity of dependents. W&I program officials annually review the criteria and apply updates to the following filing season's returns. In 2014, about 59 percent of all W&I audits—more than 516,000—were selected with a specialized computer tool called the Dependent Database, while the remainder was selected through a combination of referrals and manual selection methods.

W&I generally has established a positive environment for internal controls but could improve several areas in its audit selection procedures to support its mission. GAO found several procedures that establish a positive environment for promoting internal controls, such as ethics training. In addition, IRS has guidance to help ensure that decisions about updates to audit selection criteria are correctly implemented in its automated systems. However, W&I does not have established objectives for its audit selection process, and existing performance measures focus on audit results rather than audit selection. In addition, W&I has not defined key terms such as "fairness and integrity," as required by internal control standards. Documented objectives and key terms would help W&I hone the measures it uses to assess its audit selection efforts and bring a consistent understanding of "fairness and integrity" to audit selection staff.

GAO also found that not all elements of the selection process were appropriately documented. For example, W&I does not have clear documentation about how the three offices that select the majority of returns W&I audits interact with one another. Additionally, one guidance document notes that returns with the highest audit potential should be marked, but it does not describe how audit potential is determined or any related internal controls. Further, W&I also did not provide support showing that changes to automated audit selection processes and procedures were appropriately implemented in a timely manner. Moreover, the documentation indicates that W&I conducts an annual—rather than continuous— review of its audit selections and results as part of an annual 3-day working session. Strengthening controls in these areas would help provide greater assurance that W&I is fulfilling its mission to select tax returns with fairness and integrity. Additionally, the absence of a fully documented selection process may make it difficult for W&I to defend against accusations that it is not appropriately following its processes and procedures.

ABBREVIATIONS

CDW	Compliance Data Warehouse
DDb	Dependent Database
EITC	Earned Income Tax Credit
EOAD	Examination Operational Automation Database
ERM	Enterprise Risk Management
IRM	Internal Revenue Manual
IRS	Internal Revenue Service
IT	information technology
ITIN	Individual Taxpayer Identification Number
IVO	Integrity and Verification Operations program
OMB	Office of Management and Budget
RCPPM	Refundable Credits Policy and Program Management
RICS	Return Integrity and Compliance Services
SB/SE	Small Business/Self-Employed division
TIGTA	Tax Inspector General for Tax Administration
W&I	Wage and Investment division

December 17, 2015

The Honorable Kevin Brady
Chairman
Committee on Ways and Means
House of Representatives

The Honorable Peter J. Roskam
Chairman
Subcommittee on Oversight
Committee on Ways and Means
House of Representatives

The Internal Revenue Service's (IRS) Wage and Investment (W&I) division audited more than 516,000 individual tax returns in fiscal year 2014—accounting for 42 percent of IRS's efforts to review individual taxpayers' returns in terms of audit volume.[1] Audits help ensure that taxpayers comply with tax laws and help address the tax gap—the estimated difference between the amount of taxes that taxpayers pay voluntarily and on time and those they owe. IRS estimated that for tax year 2006, the net tax gap of $385 billion included $235 billion from underreporting of individual income tax.

W&I's broad scope and the number of taxpayers it audits raise stakes for properly selecting tax returns for audit. Unfair selection for audit could place extra burden on taxpayers and reduce the public's confidence in IRS, which could undercut voluntary tax compliance and reduce federal revenue. Unfairly selected audits also could waste IRS resources.

We recently have reported on IRS's internal controls for other IRS selection programs. For example, in July 2015, we reported that the Exempt Organizations unit within the Tax Exempt and Government Entities division had several areas where its controls were not well designed or implemented.[2] The control deficiencies increase the risk of selecting organizations for audit in an unfair manner—for example, based on an organization's religious, educational, political, or other views. We recommended that IRS take 10 actions to improve selection control design and implementation, to which IRS generally agreed. Similarly, in July and in September 2015, we found that IRS did not clearly define program objectives and key terms in its collection programs, which could undercut IRS's ability to assess risks and monitor performance.[3] We recommended that IRS improve collection controls and procedures, and periodically evaluate the controls' effectiveness. IRS generally agreed with the recommendations.

To better understand how individual tax returns are chosen for audit and whether those procedures were fair, you asked us to review W&I audit selection procedures. This report (1) describes the W&I process for selecting tax returns for audit, and (2) determines how well W&I's procedures for selecting returns for audit support its mission and goal to apply the tax law with integrity and fairness to all.

To describe the W&I process for selecting returns for audit, we reviewed documentation on program procedures from the Internal Revenue Manual (IRM) and other IRS documentation describing audit procedures. We also interviewed relevant IRS audit officials. For context, we compiled statistical information from fiscal years 2013 and 2014 about W&I audit programs from IRS's Compliance Data Warehouse—which provides a variety of tax return, enforcement, compliance, and other data—and the Examination Operational Automation Database, which contains information on audit adjustments relating to specific audit issues. For the purposes of this review, we determined that the data used in our analysis were reliable. Our data reliability assessment included reviewing relevant documentation, interviewing knowledgeable IRS officials, and reviewing the data to identify obvious errors or outliers.

To determine how well W&I's procedures for selecting tax returns for audit support its mission, we reviewed W&I's audit selection procedures and related internal controls intended to help W&I achieve its stated mission of "applying the tax law with integrity and fairness to all." We then assessed whether these relevant W&I procedures followed selected internal control standards from *Standards for Internal Control in the Federal Government*. The controls we chose applied to the processes and procedures that W&I officials described or for which they provided documentation regarding how audits were selected. We also relied on the *Internal Control Management and Evaluation Tool* to identify specific factors that could be used to operationalize the internal control standards.[4] In addition, we also reviewed Internal Revenue Service's *Strategic Plan FY2014-2017*; IRM sections related to W&I's mission statement and program objectives; IRS's policy statement for audits and information technology controls; W&I's fiscal year 2014 program letter; and other IRS documentation related to W&I's audit selection process, including internal risk assessment documents and annual meeting notes.[5] We also interviewed relevant IRS officials concerning their understanding of the mission, objectives, and internal controls for audit selection procedures. While we relied on documentation demonstrating whether the standards were addressed, we did not test whether they were systemically applied. For additional details on our scope and methodology, see appendix I.

We conducted this performance audit from October 2014 to December 2015 in accordance with generally accepted government auditing standards. Those standards require that we plan and perform the audit to obtain sufficient, appropriate evidence to provide a reasonable basis for our findings and conclusions based on our audit objectives. We believe that the evidence obtained provides a reasonable basis for our findings and conclusions based on our audit objectives.

BACKGROUND

W&I supports IRS's mission by maintaining an enforcement presence and encouraging the correct reporting of income tax to instill the highest degree of public confidence in the tax system's integrity, fairness, and efficiency. Audit programs in W&I cover mainly refundable credits on the Form 1040 U.S. Individual Income Tax Return.

All W&I's audits are correspondence audits—a type of audit conducted through the mail. Audits have two compliance effects. First, they directly detect and correct noncompliance by the audited taxpayers. Second, audits indirectly encourage nonaudited taxpayers to comply voluntarily.

W&I's audit responsibilities generally concern refundable credits claimed on individual income tax returns. A refundable credit can give taxpayers a refund even if they owe no tax and are not otherwise required to file a tax return. Nonrefundable credits also can reduce taxpayers' tax, but any excess is not refunded.

The most common refundable credit that W&I audits is the Earned Income Tax Credit (EITC), which is a benefit for working people with low to moderate income.[6] EITC will cost an estimated $58 billion in federal outlays in fiscal year 2016, according to the Office of Management and Budget (OMB). IRS measures noncompliance in claiming EITC and also uses those measures to estimate its portion of federal improper payments. EITC was the second biggest contributor to the federal government's estimated $124.7 billion in improper payments in fiscal year 2014.[7] Specifically, EITC accounted for an estimated $17.7 billion in improper payments, which is approximately 27 percent of its outlays during fiscal year 2014.[8] OMB has established guidance for federal agencies on reporting, reducing, and recovering improper payments as required by the Improper Payments Information Act of 2002, as amended.[9] Other refundable credits that W&I covers include the Additional Child Tax Credit, American Opportunity Tax Credit, and Premium Tax Credit.[10]

IRS also operates other compliance programs that may lead to tax returns being referred to the audit function but are not audit programs. Examples of these programs include the following.

- The math error program corrects certain obvious errors on tax returns at the time they are filed, such as claiming a credit above the allowed income threshold.
- The Automated Underreporter program matches income data reported on a tax return with third-party information about income and expenses provided to IRS by employers and financial institutions. Mismatches can result in IRS asking the taxpayer to successfully explain the discrepancy or pay additional tax.
- The nonfiler program uses third-party information to identify people who do not file a required tax return. Some nonfiler cases may be forwarded for audit, according to IRS officials.
- The unallowables program identifies items reported on a tax return that are specifically disallowed by law or rule and result in the tax return not being accepted by IRS. These can include taxpayers' claims of deductions, items exceeding statutory limits, or items not supported by the proper information or schedule.

In November 2014, IRS realigned its tax compliance organizations that served individual and small business taxpayers to improve efficiency and identify emerging compliance issues more quickly, as well as streamline decision making and resources in audit and collection while avoiding duplication. The realignment changed what the W&I and Small Business and Self-Employed (SB/SE) divisions audit.[11] W&I kept work focused on EITC. Most post-refund discretionary programs moved from W&I to SB/SE except EITC post-refund work. Under the realignment, W&I also took on new responsibilities, such as certain audits of returns reporting income on Schedule C Profit or Loss from Business.

Three Offices have Responsibility for Audit Selection, but Automated Programs Select the Majority of Returns that W&I Audits

Three W&I Offices Largely Determine What Returns Get Selected for Audit

W&I's audit programs are managed out of an office called Return Integrity and Compliance Services (RICS), which operates three other offices that directly or indirectly review tax return data for potential audits. These other three offices include:

- Refundable Credits Policy and Program Management (RCPPM);
- Deputy Director's Return Integrity, and Compliance Services; and
- Refundable Credits Examination Operations.

Figure 1 shows how RICS's audit offices are connected to the W&I Commissioner's office in W&I's organization.

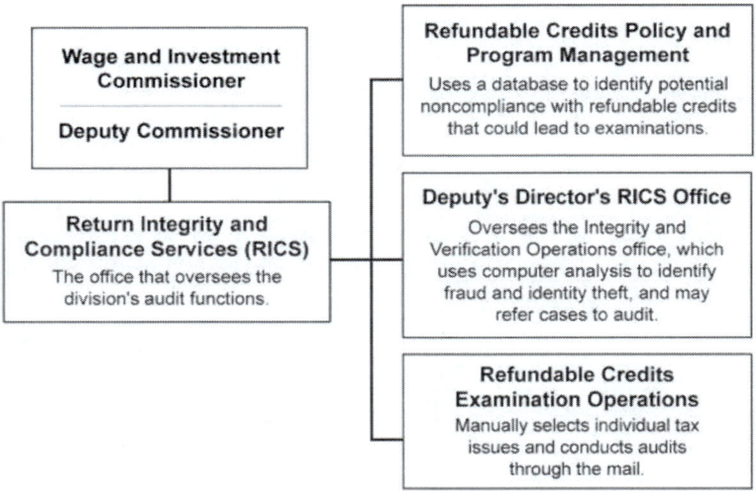

Source: GAO analysis of IRS information. | GAO-16-102.

Figure 1. Wage and Investment Division Offices Responsible for Selecting Tax Returns for Audit.

RCPPM: This office oversees refundable credit enforcement and establishes filters for computerized selection of returns for audit. The main tools RCPPM uses for selecting returns for audit are filters from the Dependent Database (DDb).[12] These filters identify returns and use risk- based scoring to select the returns. DDb creates the scores after W&I enters tax return data but before refunds are issued. Some of the rules/criteria include the use of taxpayer's dependent information, such as related children data, qualifying children claimed with multiple taxpayers, birth parents, and birth parents' Social Security numbers and dates of birth. If information from a tax return creates a high enough score, the return may be made available for audit in Refundable Credits Examination Operations. If the return is audited, letters will systemically be issued to the taxpayers asking them to explain an issue on the tax return.

W&I holds an annual 3-day working session to set and evaluate the effectiveness of its DDb filters for selecting returns for possible audit. W&I conducts analyses throughout the year in support of this meeting, which includes W&I research, the Information Technology (IT) Office, and RICS. The May 2015 working session included more than two dozen officials, including two executives. The officials review new laws and audit results to help evaluate the effectiveness of the business rules. An example of a law that W&I discussed during its annual working session included the Patient Protection and Affordable Care Act, which created the Premium Tax Credit.[13] Audit results that the officials also consider during the meeting include no-change rates, defined as the proportion of audits that resulted in no changes to the assessed tax amount for the tax return). Modifications to the selection criteria are incorporated into a unified work request for W&I's IT Office. The request is reviewed and approved by the Business Modernization Office, IT, and stakeholder division executives before programming is done to incorporate the new criteria.[14]

Deputy Director's RICS office: This office operates the Integrity and Verification Operations (IVO), which is not an audit program, but may refer returns with refundable credits for audit. IVO uses several computer systems, including DDb, to identify fraud and refund abuse across many types of taxes, including refundable credits. W&I annually reviews tolerances that IVO uses to search tax return data for potential fraud, abuse, or other noncompliance. IVO also has a program that processes leads from external stakeholder partners, such as financial institutions, state agencies, or other third parties. This program focuses on stopping fraudulent refunds from issuing and/or recovering fraudulent refunds that were issued and are identified via external sources.

Refundable Credits Examination Operations: The Refundable Credits Examination Operations office performs classification duties and conducts audits. Classification is the process of determining whether a return has potential noncompliance worth auditing and what issues should be audited. The criteria that classifiers use to decide what issues should be sent for audit are listed in IRM 4.1.5 and 4.19.11.

In W&I, classification is conducted on Form 1040x Amended Return submissions or returns that were referred from other parts of IRS. The returns referred from other parts of IRS that W&I classifies generally do not meet existing DDb criteria for return selection or were amended returns submitted to IRS on paper. Referrals from other business units are one of IRS's priority audit categories, which also includes new employee audits and mandatory work, such as nationally coordinated research projects. Once a classifier classifies the return and identifies the issues, the letter is generated and the audit is started. This inventory is not assigned to an auditor until correspondence is received. In some cases, W&I classifiers may send a return to another business unit, such as SB/SE. W&I also classifies returns filed with an Individual Tax Identification Number (ITIN) to check for tax noncompliance.[15] For example, returns that are filed with an ITIN and that meet audit referral criteria for the refundable Additional Child Tax Credit are set aside for classification.

Automated System Led to the Most W&I Audit Selections

In fiscal year 2014, DDb selected 59 percent of W&I's audit inventory, as shown in figure 2. The next largest source of audits was referrals from IVO. Manual classification of ITIN and amended returns, as well as other referrals, together accounted for a relatively smaller fraction of the overall number of W&I audits in fiscal year 2014—meaning that most W&I case selection was computer driven. W&I audits resulted in $2.5 billion in recommended additional tax in fiscal year 2014, down from $3.3 billion in fiscal year 2013. W&I also had $49 million and $69 million in revenue protection in 2014 and 2013 respectively.[16] IRS did not have reliable data to analyze the number of audits or assessments in prior years. However, these totals include audits of issues that W&I is no longer responsible for addressing, such as referrals from state agencies. IRS officials told us that they did not have reliable data for the most recent fiscal year at the time of our audit.

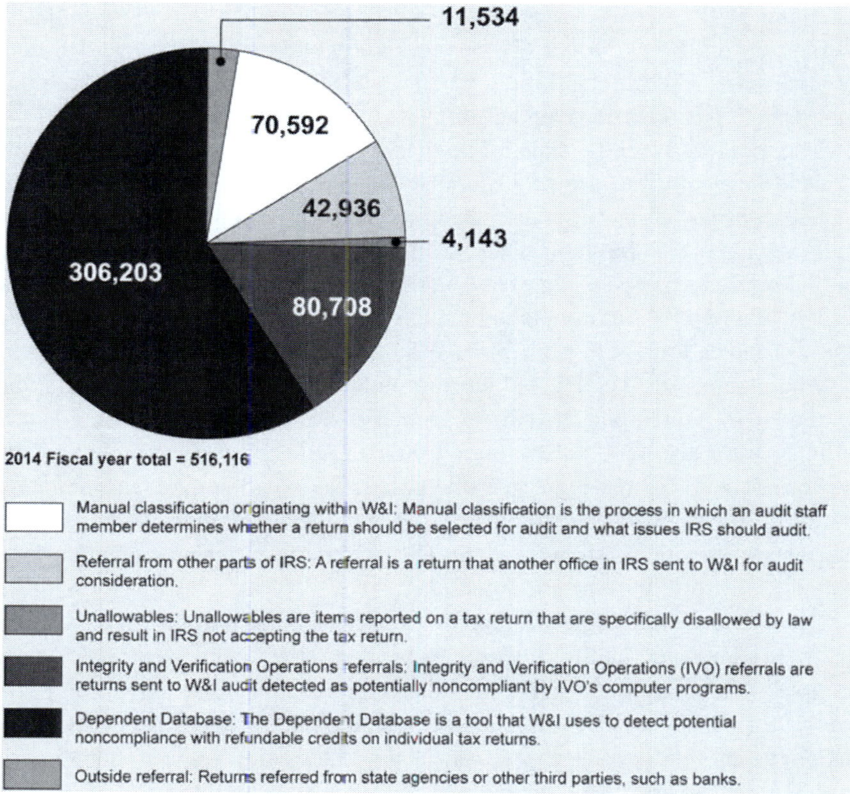

Source: GAO analysis of IRS information. | GAO-16-102

Note: Figure includes audits that W&I conducted in the past but no longer does because of a 2014 realignment of audit responsibilities at IRS. IRS did not have reliable fiscal year 2015 data available in time for this report.

Figure 2. Number of Wage and Investment (W&I) Audits by Selection Method, Fiscal Year 2014.

Audit Start Management Effectively Acts as an Additional Return Selection Method

In addition to setting criteria for automated systems to apply to tax return data, managers at W&I's headquarters set the number of audit starts at the beginning of the fiscal year and make weekly adjustments in the number of returns selected for audit that will be worked by audit staff. Because IRS does not audit every return identified by the automated systems, this workload management is a form of audit selection.

The tool that W&I officials use to manage the audit starts is the work plan, a spreadsheet with the projected number of audits by type of tax that W&I managers write before cases are selected at the beginning of the fiscal year. Audit managers use the spreadsheet to allocate returns audit starts based on the goals W&I has set for closing cases, work already in process, and the available number of auditors. Auditors then generally work returns on a first in, first out basis. At the end of fiscal year 2015, W&I reported having 683 tax examiners of which about 584 conducted correspondence audits and the others did support work, including taxpayers' requests to reconsider previous audit findings. W&I also reported having 47 tax compliance officers. In developing the work plan, W&I managers said they also take overall compliance strategies for specific refundable credits into account that include audit as one component. Figure 3 shows where RICS's audit processes operate in a simplified illustration of return processing.

Beyond available resources, another measure that W&I officials say they use to review their audit selection methods is the no-change rate. As an example, W&I requested changing criteria on qualifying children for EITC reviews for fiscal year 2015 to reduce no-change rates. Audits that end with no change to the reported tax assessment on the return impose burdens on compliant taxpayers. W&I officials also said a low no-change rate reflects more efficient use of IRS resources. IRS officials said they calculated W&I's overall no-change rate as 10.1 percent for work compiled through September of fiscal year 2015, with the no-change rate specifically for DDb selections under the realignment as 12.5 percent.

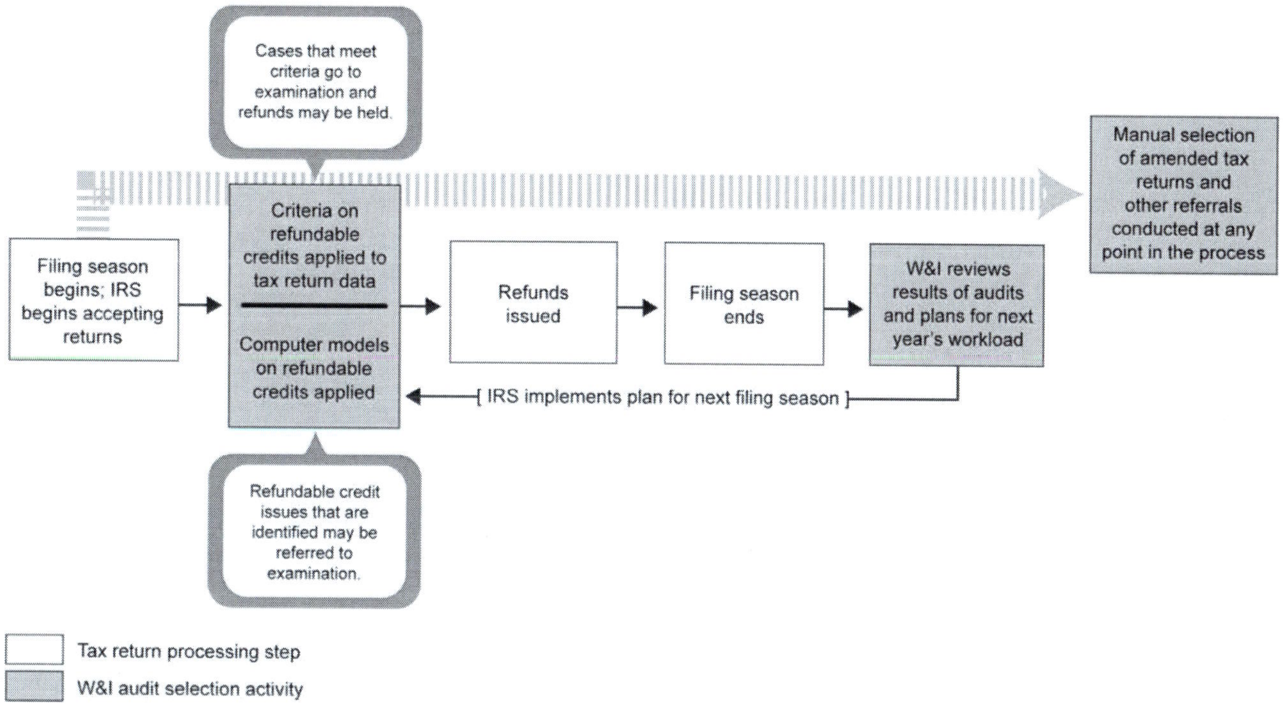

Source: GAO analysis of IRS information. | GAO-16-102.

Figure 3. Individual Income Tax Return Processing Sequence and When Return Integrity and Compliance Programs Select Returns to Audit.

W&I Designed and Implemented Certain Controls for Audit Selection, but Should Develop and Strengthen Others to Reduce Risk of Unfair Practices

Implementation of an effective internal control system can improve accountability in achieving an entity's mission. As set forth in *Standards for Internal Control in the Federal Government*, internal control is a major part of managing an organization as it comprises the plans, methods, and procedures used to meet missions, goals, and objectives, which support performance-based management.[17] In addition, internal controls help agency program managers achieve desired results and provide reasonable assurance through the effectiveness and efficiency of operations, among other things. Further, internal control is not one singular event, but a series of actions and activities that occur throughout an entity's operations and on an ongoing basis. Examples of internal controls include establishing clear, consistent agency objectives, documenting significant events, and ongoing monitoring. While W&I has documented how some of its procedures meet the internal control standards, we found some potential issues that increase the risk that W&I audit selection activities may not fully contribute to its mission to treat all taxpayers fairly and with integrity.

W&I Generally has Established a Positive Environment for Promoting Internal Controls

Internal control standards require that management and employees establish and maintain a positive and supportive environment toward internal control and conscientious management. Several key factors affect the control environment such as ethical values maintained and demonstrated by management and staff, management's philosophy towards performance-based management, and delegation of authority and responsibility, among others.

We found several IRS procedures that demonstrated some factors of a positive environment for promoting internal controls.[18] First, IRS's IRM includes various ethics guidance for all staff.[19] For example, IRM cross-references federal and IRS agency ethics regulations that include 14 principles of ethical conduct, such as conflicts of interest and political activities of staff.[20] IRS requires all managers to hold an annual ethics discussion with their staff and all IRS staff to certify that they attended the discussion. While the code of conduct does not specifically address audit selection, IRS provided sufficient documentation to demonstrate that staff should be aware of the need to act ethically when conducting their duties—such as by not letting personal biases affect audit selection. In addition, W&I officials stated that they were not aware of any staff responsible for audit selection violating the code of conduct.

INTERNAL CONTROL STANDARD: CONTROL ENVIRONMENT

A positive control environment is the foundation for all other standards.

Source: GAO. | GAO-16-102.

Second, IRS staff are rated annually on their performance, including whether they met the retention standard for the fair and equitable treatment of taxpayers.[21] IRM requires supervisors to brief staff on what types of behaviors would meet or not meet the standard.[22] For instance, if a staff member's communications with taxpayers are professional and courteous and accurately state the facts, the standard would be met. While the performance appraisal criteria do not specifically address fairness for audit selection, IRS has documentation to demonstrate that staff should conduct their duties according to the standard.[23]

Third, W&I has clearly assigned authority and responsibility for its audit selection processes. W&I demonstrated this by providing a list of (1) IRS stakeholders who participated in W&I's annual meetings to discuss any revisions to audit selection criteria for fiscal year 2015, 2) program analysts involved in modifying audit selection rules, and 3) Submissions Processing staff tasked with referring returns that meet certain criteria to staff classifying tax returns, such as amended individual tax returns that include certain tax credits.[24] In addition, staff who are responsible for modifying audit selection criteria do not audit returns. Similarly, staff who classify a return cannot audit that return.

Fourth, staff that manually classify amended returns for potential audit are to receive training to help them maintain a level of competence necessary for assigned duties. Other IRS staff responsible for revising W&I criteria used in automated programs do not receive any formal training in revising the criteria.

W&I officials told us they believed that most of these staff are well versed and proficient in their respective areas of tax law because they are either IRS executives or senior managers with at least 20 years of experience. They said that such staff have had years of related training in specialized areas for their former positions (e.g., revenue agents and department managers) and use their experience as well as feedback from W&I staff involved in the audits, research data, and audit results to help inform their decision in revising audit selection criteria.

W&I Has Not Clearly Defined Key Terms and Program-Level Objectives to Evaluate Whether Its Audit Selection Process is Meeting Its Mission

Internal control standards call for specific terms to be clearly defined and set forth so they can be easily understood. Management should define program objectives that align with an entity's mission, strategic plan, goals, and requirements of applicable laws and regulations. Clearly defined objectives can enhance program effectiveness and efficiency. Documenting objectives allow agency officials and staff to have a consistent understanding of the organization's purpose.

INTERNAL CONTROL STANDARD: DEFINE OBJECTIVES

Program objectives are to be clearly defined in measurable terms to enable the design of internal control. Specific terms should be fully defined and clearly set forth so they can be easily understood at all levels of the organization.

Source: GAO. | GAO-16-102.

W&I has not clearly defined, documented, or communicated key terms. For example, while the concepts of "fairness" and "integrity" are highlighted in IRS's mission and policy statements and W&I's mission statement, W&I has not defined or documented fairness and integrity, particularly for audit selection.[25] As a result, each staff member is left to define these terms.[26]

W&I officials shared views on how fairness and integrity might be defined for audit selection. For fairness, a senior W&I official informally defined it as having a low no-change rate and incorporating eligibility requirements as outlined by the Internal Revenue Code or other legislation into audit selection criteria. In addition, W&I officials said they believed that W&I's audit selection process is fair because all individual tax returns that run through DDb are scored by the same audit selection criteria. Further, Submissions Processing staff apply audit criteria for all amended returns, which may require classification by classifiers if they are flagged for potential audit. For integrity, W&I officials highlighted all of IRS's six core values, including honesty and integrity, which focuses on upholding "the public trust" and being "honest and forthright in all internal and external dealings."[27] However, they did not indicate how they know integrity is provided in audit selection. As a result, by not communicating a clear definition of fairness and integrity to all staff involved in audit selection, W&I is vulnerable to inconsistent selections.

In addition, W&I has not established program-level objectives on the selection of returns for audit that support its and IRS's shared mission of applying the tax law with integrity and fairness to all. Rather, W&I has four broad audit goals, including:

- measuring the degree of voluntary compliance on filed returns;
- reducing noncompliance by identifying and cost-effectively allocating resources to those returns most in need of audit;
- conducting timely and quality audits of tax returns; and
- making quality contacts to determine the correct taxable amount.[28]

These audit goals do not refer to fairness and integrity because these terms have not been defined by IRS or W&I. W&I officials confirmed that they do not have program-level objectives for how returns are selected. However, W&I has developed fiscal year 2016 activities for its annual operations plan that has references to potential objectives.[29] For instance, one of RCPPM's action item focuses on RICS reviewing and creating workload selection filters intended to ensure fairness and integrity, running all individual tax returns against such filters, and pursuing audits with high probable changes with the intent of reducing no-change rates.

Internal control standards also require management to establish activities to monitor performance measures and indicators. Performance measures and targets are used to compare actual results to planned performance. Without clearly defined program-level objectives on its audit selection process, W&I cannot measure whether its selection criteria are meeting its mission of applying the tax law with fairness and integrity. Existing performance measures focus on audit results rather than audit selection. W&I officials stated that the no-change rate could be viewed as a performance measure to evaluate whether W&I was meeting its mission of applying the tax law with integrity and fairness to all. W&I's stated goal is to decrease the no-change rate to assure that the right taxpayers are claiming a credit, for example, based on its selection criteria. W&I officials stated that they use different no-change rates by issue type, such as the Earned Income Tax Credit, and strive to keep them as low as possible. However, W&I has not created indicators to evaluate what no-change rate is good or bad, or what rate would indicate fair selections. We reported in June 2014 that IRS did not document criteria on how its managers were to use performance data, such as the no-change rate, or to make program decisions, such as the number of audits or tax issues to audit.[30]

Lack of Clear Program Objectives Creates Challenges for Effective Risk Assessment in Audit Selection

Internal control standards state that management needs to identify and analyze relevant internal and external risks, and then decide how to manage those risks; a precondition to risk assessment is the establishment of clear program objectives. The first and most critical step of risk assessment is risk identification. Management should have well- documented procedures for regularly identifying internal and external risks to program objectives and procedures, such as in short- and long- term forecasting and strategic planning.

INTERNAL CONTROL STANDARD: ASSESS RISKS TO PROGRAM OBJECTIVES

Management is to comprehensively identify internal and external risks and determine relative risk rankings on a scheduled and periodic basis.

Source: GAO. | GAO-16-102.

Because W&I does not have clearly formulated and communicated program objectives for audit selection, W&I cannot fully implement a process to identify potential risks in its audit selection process. Without risk identification and assessments linked to program objectives, vulnerabilities may go unaddressed, resulting in unfair case selection, decreased dollars collected, greater noncompliance, or other negative program effects.

Additionally, W&I does not have reasonable assurance that it is appropriately assessing risk in its audit selection process in two areas in which W&I officials believe the risks are low. First, W&I officials said that they do not think certain internal control elements related to risk assessment—such as downsizing operations or changing operating processes—affect the audit selection process; however the federal internal control tool views these factors as applicable. Second, IRS had identified no risk of bias for automated audit selection programs because the programs compare data on a taxpayer's return with third-party data. Robust internal controls to address risks that threaten the automated selection criteria are especially important because automated programs select the majority of returns that W&I audits.

IRS is implementing an Enterprise Risk Management (ERM) program to consider risks more systematically across IRS. As we recently reported, IRS implemented ERM, among other reasons, to serve as an early- warning system to identify and address emerging challenges and address them before they affect operations. According to IRS's Chief Risk Officer, the goal is to embed risk management principles and practices into the daily operations of the business units and integrate long-standing processes into the new, more holistic ERM approach. Since the implementation of the ERM process is ongoing, it is too early to determine the effectiveness of ERM in identifying and managing risk.[31] ERM is intended to help organizations in setting strategy to consider risk and how much risk the organization is willing to accept. According to IRS officials, ERM is broader in scope than internal controls, focusing on agency-wide risks. It is important for agencies to assess risk at both the agency-wide and the program level.

W&I Assigns and Communicates Internal Control Responsibilities to Managers, but not to Its Non-Managers, Raising the Potential Risk for Unfair Selection

We found that IRS has various procedures that convey the importance of internal controls at the managerial level, such as IRM guidance on monitoring internal controls, an annual managerial self-assessment of adherence to internal controls, and a classification quality review process. To the extent that managers report deficiencies and W&I uses the results, the annual self-assessment of IRS's internal controls can provide assurance that the importance of internal controls is understood at the managerial level. W&I officials provided an example of a completed fiscal year 2014 self-assessment that included a manager's sign-off of a reasonable assurance that IRS's controls are effective and operating as intended.[32] However, beyond "yes" and "not applicable" responses, the documentation did not provide any detailed responses on the internal controls assessed and their relationship to the audit selection process.

INTERNAL CONTROL STANDARD: INFORMATION AND COMMUNICATIONS

Information should be communicated to management and others within the agency who need it and within a time frame that enables them to carry out their own internal control and other responsibilities.

Source: GAO. | GAO-16-102.

In response to how internal control responsibilities were communicated to all staff, including non-managers, W&I officials stated that internal controls are built into their processes, such as the annual meetings, staffing designations and tasks, automated systems, risk identification and assessments, and monitoring. In addition, they said that the annual self-assessment process requires managers to certify that the operations and staff they manage are in compliance with internal controls. The fiscal year 2014 self-assessment includes a question regarding whether managers communicated policies on a routine basis that enabled staff to meet and understand their internal control and other responsibilities effectively. Beyond a "yes" response by one of W&I's managers, IRS did not provide evidence that W&I directly assigned and communicated internal control responsibilities to non-managers, such as program analysts and classifiers who are tasked with revising or applying audit selection criteria, respectively. By not relaying information on internal control responsibilities to all employees, W&I has less assurance that its employees understand internal controls and increases the risk of not being aware of potential internal control issues that could result in unfair audit selection.

W&I Has Guidance for Automated Systems to Control Access and Modifications to Its Audit Selection Criteria

Federal internal control standards require a variety of control activities for information processing, such as controlling access to data, files, and programs. In addition, access to resources should be limited to authorized individuals, and accountability for their use should be assigned and maintained. Access rights are used to implement security policies that determine what a user can do after being allowed into the system, such as allowing the user to read or write to a certain file or directory. Maintaining access rights is an important aspect of administering system security. In addition to access controls, other controls should be in place to ensure the integrity of an organization's information. These controls can include, but are not limited to, policies, procedures, and techniques for securely configuring information systems with software updates.

We found IRM guidance that specifies procedures to restrict access to authorized users as well as various software testing mechanisms. Specifically, IRM sections on information technology (IT) security documented access to data, files, and programs for modifying IT systems, including those that cover W&I's audit selection criteria. For example, IRS uses a process to register all users for access to any IRS IT resource when their access is authorized by the user's manager. By obtaining such access, IT programmers can utilize the official change management system to add new or modify W&I audit selection criteria that are based on the unified work request that is approved by IRS management.[33] However, we reported in March 2015 that IRS had not updated the security authorization for IRS's access request and approval system to reflect significant changes made to the operating environment.[34] As a result, we recommended that IRS update the security authorization for the access request as well as the approval system to reflect the significant changes to the operating environment. In response to this recommendation, IRS agreed to provide corrective action plans where appropriate.[35] In addition, the Tax Inspector General for Tax Administration (TIGTA) has an ongoing audit related to the request and approval process in obtaining access to IRS systems.[36]

INTERNAL CONTROL STANDARD: CONTROL ACTIVITIES FOR INFORMATION SYSTEMS

Access security control protects the systems and network from inappropriate access and unauthorized use. Application control is designed to help ensure completeness, accuracy, authorization, and validity of all transactions during application processing.

Source: GAO. | GAO-16-102.

IRM has a section on testing procedures to ensure accurate revisions are made, such as modifying W&I's audit selection criteria.[37] IT officials also provided other guidance, such as the IT Test Reference Guide, to address how new or revised software is to be thoroughly tested and approved. IT officials provided examples of output reports to show how DDb modifications to W&I audit selection criteria were tested, approved, and working as designed.

IRS has Documented Policies to Support Internal Controls but Shows Weaknesses in Documenting Aspects of Audit Selection

Internal control standards state that documentation should clearly identify procedures and should allow agency officials and staff to understand the purpose of internal control procedures and be readily available for audit. Documenting procedures is evidence that the right controls are identified and that those procedures are capable of being communicated to those responsible for their performance, and capable of being monitored and evaluated.

INTERNAL CONTROL STANDARD: DOCUMENT CONTROLS TO ADDRESS RISKS TO PROGRAM OBJECTIVES

Procedures should be clearly documented to ensure that management's plans, policies, and procedures are sufficiently and fully carried out.

Source: GAO. | GAO-16-102.

IRS has documented some agency-wide policies to support internal controls, but these are not always linked to W&I's audit selection process. For example, as noted previously, IRS provided sufficient documentation to demonstrate that staff should be aware of the need to act ethically when conducting their duties, such as not letting personal biases affect their work (e.g. selecting returns for audit). Other IRS policies—including the retention standard—reference the fair and equitable treatment of taxpayers in general, but do not consistently reference audit selection in particular.

We also found some weaknesses in documenting parts of the audit selection plan. W&I has workload selection templates that describe the methods that IRS uses to identify and select tax returns for audit. The templates are intended to explain how W&I determined, tested, and approved the steps involved in each method, as well as what types of staff and functions are involved. While some elements of the selection process are described in detail in the workload selection templates, not all elements of the selection process—ranging from determining audit potential to inter-office interactions—are covered.

For example, one workload selection template notes that returns with the highest audit potential are marked, but it does not describe how audit potential is determined. Additionally, the workload selection templates do not describe how the systems and processes described in the templates are related. For example, W&I lacks clear documentation about how the three offices which select the majority of returns W&I audits—Refundable Credits Policy and Program Management; the Deputy Director's Return Integrity, and Compliance Services; and Refundable Credits Examination Operations—interact with one another. The lack of comprehensive documentation to describe W&I's audit selection process results in less assurance that these processes effectively address risks. Additionally, the absence of a fully documented selection process may make it difficult for W&I to defend against accusations that it is not appropriately following its processes and procedures, since the incomplete documentation makes it difficult to clearly communicate about how audit selection works.

Monitoring Procedures do not Ensure Effective Implementation of Corrective Actions

According to internal control standards, program managers should have a strategy and establish procedures for ongoing monitoring to assure the effectiveness of its control activities, and that deficiencies found during separate evaluations should be resolved in a timely manner. Monitoring involves management assessing the design and operational effectiveness of internal control systems as well as ensuring that corrective actions are effectively implemented in a timely manner. Serious deficiencies and internal control problems should be reported to top management in a timely manner. Managers and supervisors should know their responsibilities for internal control and the need to make control and control monitoring part of their regular operating processes.

INTERNAL CONTROL STANDARD: MONITOR CONTROLS

Internal control design should assure that ongoing monitoring of controls occurs in the course of normal operations.

Source: GAO-16-102.

While W&I's policy is clear that internal control issues should be reported to the next level of management, the mechanism to elevate potential internal control issues to management is limited. The IRM states that a problem in the design or operation of an internal control should be reported to the next level of management as a significant deficiency.[38] It does not, however, specify how non-managers should report it or that it should be reported in a timely manner. The form that W&I staff would use to report such deficiencies in the automated filters used for return selection—the Compliance Data Environment Production Filter Modification Approval form—includes space for submitting modification requests for the automated filters, but not for reporting internal control deficiencies that do not have a proposed solution. The form also states that the reason for modification should be self-explanatory, which may not appropriately highlight the deficiency the modification seeks to address. W&I officials said that IRS has no guidance beyond the instructions on the form to report deficiencies and that no deficiencies have been identified with this form.

W&I officials subsequently identified general ways in which staff could report internal control deficiencies. They said that staff can send e-mails directly to the Commissioner, submit help desk tickets for IT issues, provide feedback during a regularly-scheduled forum, make a submission to the "I suggest" program to improve a program or process, or supply feedback on IRM sections. When asked to provide examples of employees elevating potential internal control issues, W&I officials also provided examples of internal control issues identified during the monitoring process.

This limitation in the reporting mechanism—including the limited examples of staff reporting deficiencies—increases the risk that W&I would not know about a potential deficiency that staff perceive or experience. Without a clear means of elevating possible internal control deficiencies to top management in a timely manner, W&I does not have reasonable assurance that concerns noticed by an employee are reported appropriately or in a timely manner.

In addition, we found some limitations in the timeliness of W&I's monitoring. W&I officials said that, at the beginning of each filing season, a team made up of experienced analysts and managers reviews selections and notices generated from the new programming to ensure programming is working as intended, and that the generated notices are correct. They also said that they continuously monitor audit selections and results to ensure that implemented corrective actions were appropriate.

However, the documentation indicates that it is an annual—rather than continuous—review as part of W&I's annual 3-day working session that included evaluating the effectiveness of its criteria for selecting returns for possible audit. Further, W&I did not clearly document what corrective actions, if any, were taken and how they were implemented in response to the deficiencies it identified at the annual working session. W&I officials provided documentation of issues identified with the Premium Tax Credit; however, the deadlines for actions items were all at least 6 months past, and W&I did not provide support that those changes were appropriately implemented. Because of this, W&I lacks reasonable assurance that the issues were addressed in an appropriate or timely manner and that they have been sufficiently resolved. Without ensuring that it has sufficient controls to identify deficiencies and take necessary corrective action, W&I may be missing opportunities to ensure that the changes work as intended and lower the risk of selecting audits unfairly.

CONCLUSIONS

W&I auditors have interacted with hundreds of thousands of taxpayers and assessed billions of dollars in tax changes, making W&I's mission of applying the tax law with fairness and integrity all the more critical. Failure to accomplish that mission could undermine the public's confidence in the tax system, waste resources, and burden taxpayers. Properly designed and maintained internal controls for audit selection can help W&I better assure its mission. While we found that W&I had implemented some internal controls over its array of audit selection processes, we also identified a series of internal control weaknesses that reduce the assurance that current or future audit.

Most importantly, IRS lacks clearly defined and documented program-level objectives, performance measures, indicators, and definitions of key concepts such as fairness, reducing the assurance that W&I employees are treating taxpayers equally. Without defining, documenting, and communicating to staff these aspects of internal control, IRS cannot know whether it is meeting its and W&I's shared mission of applying the tax law with fairness and integrity to all taxpayers. W&I's use of the no-change rate could be viewed as a performance measure, but it is not sufficient to assure that the audit selection criteria are fair. Having program-level objectives, performance measures, indicators, and definitions that link to its mission and goals would enhance W&I's ability assure that its audit selection processes are fair and have integrity.

Having program-level objectives for audit selection in place is a precondition to developing a risk assessment strategy for audit selection, which W&I has not adopted. With an effective risk assessment strategy for audit selection, W&I could gauge potential internal and external risks that may hinder its ability to meet its mission of treating taxpayers fairly and equally. Such a strategy would increase the assurance that W&I is appropriately selecting returns for audit, consistent with its mission.

We also found opportunities for improvement in other areas. First, W&I has not communicated internal control responsibilities to all staff tasked with audit selection, including non-managers and classifiers who revise or apply audit selection criteria, respectively. Second, W&I does not have complete documentation its audit selection procedures; doing so would improve the assurance that W&I staff have a common understanding of how the selection process work and their role in the process. Third, while W&I's policy is clear that internal control issues should be reported to the next level of management, the mechanism to elevate potential internal control issues to management is limited. Lastly, W&I did not provide support that changes to audit selection processes and procedures were appropriately monitored and implemented in a timely manner. Taking such actions to address these areas would help provide W&I reasonable assurance that its audit selection criteria are fair.

Recommendations for Executive Action

To help ensure W&I meets its mission and selects audits fairly and with integrity, we recommend that the Commissioner of Internal Revenue take the following seven actions:

- Clearly define and document: (1) key terms such as "fairness"; and (2) W&I program level objectives, performance measures, and indicators for audit selection to evaluate whether the audit selection process is meeting its mission of applying the tax law with integrity and fairness to all.
- Clearly communicate these terms, objectives, measures, and indicators to all staff involved in the selection of returns for audit.
- Incorporate the new objective(s) into W&I risk assessments done for audit selection processes.
- Ensure that internal control responsibilities are communicated and documented for all employees, including non-managers, tasked with revising or applying W&I audit selection criteria for potential audits.
- Develop and implement procedures to ensure that all criteria or methods used in programs to select returns for audit are consistently documented and approved.
- Develop and document a clear means for IRS staff members to promptly elevate to top management possible internal control issues related to audit selection in a timely manner.
- Develop, document, and implement additional monitoring procedures to ensure audit selection controls and corrective actions are implemented in a timely manner.

Agency Comments and Our Evaluation

We provided a draft of this report to the Commissioner of Internal Revenue for review and comment. The Deputy Commissioner for Services and Enforcement provided written comments, including planned actions to implement each of our recommendations, dated November 23, 2015, which are summarized below and reprinted in appendix II. In an email received November 24, 2015, the Deputy Commissioner indicated through the IRS Office of Audit Coordination that IRS generally agreed with our seven recommendations. The enclosure to IRS's letter listed specific actions planned to implement the recommendations.

IRS stated in its letter that the concept of fairness has both a collective and individual component: (1) W&I pursues those individuals who fail to comply with their tax obligations to ensure fairness to those who do and to promote public confidence in the tax system; and (2) it discharges its responsibilities with a focus on taxpayer rights. IRS can build on these components to clarify how they relate to return selection, especially when the components also cover what happens after return selection, such as when pursuing noncompliance and interacting with taxpayers during the audit. Documenting these clarifications in its definition, as well as the examples of fair selections, would help staff involved in return selection to know the specific actions that they should take to produce selections that meet IRS's definition of fairness.

We highlight this clarification because the letter discusses various features of IRS's audit program—such as existing objectives, measures, and definitions of key concepts—that IRS stated relate to fair selection. We agree that having these features is important. However, as our report discusses, these features cited in IRS's letter do not clarify what fair selection of returns for audit entails and how IRS would know whether fair selections are occurring, unless a taxpayer or other individual raises a question about the fairness of return selection. IRS's commitment to applying tax law with fairness and integrity is contained in its mission statement, as discussed in our report, but our recommendations focus on clearly explaining how that aspect of the mission is operationalized for audit selection.

IRS identified actions that specifically reflected or were generally consistent with four of the recommendations we made. These include our recommendation on communicating the definition of terms such as fairness as well as related objectives, measures, and indicators to all staff involved in audit selection; incorporating any new selection objectives into the risk assessment process that IRS would modify in fulfilling our recommendation on defining fairness; communicating and documenting internal control responsibilities to all staff involved in audit selection; and developing a means for IRS staff to elevate internal control concerns about audit selection.

For our recommendation on defining and documenting "fairness" for return selection activities, IRS's letter listed a number of ways in which it believes the selection process is fair. For example, IRS said that its audit selections are fair because IRS policies state that audit selections should be fair and that taxpayer rights should be a prime focus. IRS's letter also cited its reliance on rules and automation rather than human intervention and its desire to select the most noncompliant returns. While striving to be fair and respectful of taxpayer rights as well as to weed out selection bias or selections that focus on less noncompliant returns is important, IRS has not provided a formal definition of what fairness entails. As a result, individuals are left to define it for themselves.

Similarly, this recommendation also focused on defining and documenting related objectives, measures, and indicators for audit selection. IRS stated that it will review these areas to further ensure that audit selection meets its mission to apply the tax law with integrity and fairness. As discussed in our report, existing IRS objectives and measures did not allow IRS to evaluate whether its selection decisions were fair. We believe IRS should develop at least one objective and measure that reflects its definition of fairness. Doing so would better enable IRS to clarify how it operationalizes fairness in the selection process and assess whether its actions are meeting that objective.

In regard to our recommendation on developing and implementing procedures to ensure that all criteria or methods used in programs to select returns for audit are consistently documented and approved, IRS stated that it has procedures in place to document criteria and methods used in return selection. However, we found instances, discussed in our report, in which IRS's documentation was not specific to return selection as well as instances in which procedures were not fully documented. Incomplete documentation makes it difficult for IRS to clearly communicate how audit selection works and defend against accusations that it is not appropriately following its processes and procedures. IRS also stated that it would review existing procedures to ensure consistent documentation and approval. Our report shows evidence of this need, such as being able to show how the selection criteria and methods were used consistently.

For our recommendation on having additional procedures for monitoring audit selection controls and corrective actions, IRS stated that it will review the processes in place for documentation and timely implementation of selection controls and corrective actions to further ensure the controls and actions are implemented in a timely manner. However, our report indicated a need to do more than a review by developing additional monitoring procedures.

Jessica Lucas-Judy
Acting Director, Tax Issues
Strategic Issues

APPENDIX I: OBJECTIVES, SCOPE, AND METHODOLOGY

This report (1) describes the Wage and Investment (W&I) process for selecting tax returns for audit; and (2) determines how well W&I's procedures for selecting tax returns for audit support its mission and goal to apply the tax law with integrity and fairness to all.

To describe the W&I process for selecting returns for review and audit, we reviewed documentation on program procedures from the Internal Revenue Manual (IRM) and Internal Revenue Service (IRS) documents describing audit procedures. We also interviewed IRS officials who oversee or who work on W&I's audit selection process. For context, we compiled statistical information for fiscal years 2013 and 2014 about W&I audit program closures from IRS's Compliance Data Warehouse (CDW) and Examination Operational Automation Database (EOAD). CDW provides a variety of tax return, enforcement, compliance and other data. EOAD has information on the type of issue audited. Our data reliability assessment included reviewing relevant documentation, interviewing knowledgeable IRS officials, and reviewing the data to identify obvious errors or outliers. Based on our testing of the data and review of documentation and interviews, we determined that these data were reliable for the purposes of this report. We categorized the data by project codes with input from W&I audit officials. Because of the recent realignment of audit duties among divisions, some of the project codes in our analysis—such as those associated with the Discretionary Exam Business Rules—are no longer worked by W&I.

To determine how well W&I's procedures for selecting tax returns for audit support its mission, we reviewed W&I's audit selection procedures and related internal controls intended to help W&I achieve its stated mission of "applying the tax law with integrity and fairness to all."[39] We then assessed whether these relevant W&I procedures followed selected internal control standards from *Standards for Internal Control in the Federal Government*.[40] We also interviewed relevant IRS officials concerning their understanding of W&I's mission, objectives, and internal controls related to W&I's audit selection. In addition, we reviewed the Internal Revenue Service's *Strategic Plan FY2014-2017*, IRM sections related to W&I's mission statement and program objectives, IRS's policy statement for audits, information technology controls, W&I's fiscal year 2014 program letter, and other IRS documentation related to W&I's audit selection process, including internal risk assessment documents and annual meeting notes.[41]

To determine which internal control standards were most relevant for our review, we used the five internal control standards in *Standards for Internal Control in the Federal Government* as primary criteria and used our *Internal Control Management and Evaluation Tool* to identify specific factors that could be used to operationalize the internal control standards, in conjunction with observations from our preliminary audit work.[42] We assessed whether W&I's audit selection process addressed the selected internal control standards by reviewing documentation and interviewing IRS officials familiar with the selection process. The controls we chose applied to the processes and procedures that W&I officials described or for which they provided documentation regarding how audits were selected. While we relied on documentation demonstrating whether the standards were addressed, we did not test whether they were systemically applied.

To determine IRS's definition of fairness and integrity as it applied to W&I's audit selection, we reviewed W&I's mission statement and other documentation related to how W&I selects audits for examination and interviewed relevant IRS officials concerning their understanding of how integrity and fairness applies to W&I audit selection activities.

We conducted this performance audit from October 2014 to December 2015 in accordance with generally accepted government auditing standards. Those standards require that we plan and perform the audit to obtain sufficient, appropriate evidence to provide a reasonable basis for our findings and conclusions based on our audit objectives. We believe that the evidence obtained provides a reasonable basis for our findings and conclusions based on our audit objectives.

APPENDIX II: COMMENTS FROM THE INTERNAL REVENUE SERVICE

DEPARTMENT OF THE TREASURY
INTERNAL REVENUE SERVICE
WASHINGTON, D.C. 20224

DEPUTY COMMISSIONER

November 23, 2015

Ms. Jessica Lucas-Judy
Acting Director, Tax Issues
U.S. Government Accountability Office
441 G Street, N.W.
Washington, DC 20548

Dear Ms. Lucas-Judy:

Thank you for the opportunity to comment on the draft report titled *IRS Return Selection: Wage and Investment Division Should Define Audit Objectives and Refine Other Internal Controls* (GAO 451128). The Wage and Investment Division (W&I) has primary responsibility within the IRS for planning, coordinating, and delivering the annual filing season. Accordingly, its operations are aligned around that task and the Compliance function, responsible for selecting and auditing tax returns, is no exception. Because the W&I compliance program is a pillar of support for the filing season, its process for evaluating tax returns for fraud or non-compliance and selecting those that require additional review, or audit, is a rules-based system that evaluates the merits of each return based on the information contained thereon. The process is objective and is not subject to influence or selection bias that could result when selections are based on individual judgment. The rules-based scoring models are based on eligibility criteria established by legislation. Data matched against these filters is based on information provided on the face of the return and information provided by other government agencies, such as the Social Security Administration and the Department of Health and Human Services.

We are pleased that the Government Accountability Office has recognized the positive environment for internal controls fostered within W&I. We believe the current audit selection process, existing internal controls, and enhancement planned for implementation in 2016 provide more than reasonable assurance that audit selections are fair and are made with integrity. In the W&I Compliance sphere, the concept of fairness has both a collective and individual component. The IRS takes into account the responsibilities and obligations that all taxpayers share, we pursue those individuals who fail to comply with their tax obligations to ensure fairness to those who do and to promote public confidence in our tax system, and we discharge these important responsibilities with a focus on taxpayer rights, as embodied in the Taxpayer Bill of Rights (TBOR) and formally adopted by IRS.

The entire foundation of our selection processes is designed to objectively select returns with the highest probability of noncompliance by relying on a combination of automated processes, historical data, scoring mechanisms, and data-driven algorithms; and the entire selection process operates under a comprehensive set of checks and balances and safeguards, all aimed at delivering a process that is fair and equitable by design. Specifically, the compliance program is designed to identify and select for review those returns with the highest likelihood of being incorrect, either due to error or fraud. Although selective criteria is used to segregate those returns with the greatest potential for error, the criteria is applied uniformly to all tax returns with the scoring results based on the information presented within the four corners of the return. Fairness and equitable treatment is further incorporated into the process with respect to the scoring and selection criteria developed prior to the Filing Season.

Fairness and equity in the selection process is further promoted by the fact that most selections are automated. There is no human intervention in the process. Any changes done to selection criteria are done well in advance of returns being filed. A strong separation of duties is also in place throughout the process. The employees who examine the selected returns are individuals who have not been involved with development of selection rules, planning or any rule based programming. Updates and refinements to the automated rules are conducted annually so that any programing can be completed prior to the commencement of the upcoming Filing Season. Unified Work Requests (UWR) have to be done by a certain date in order for the programming to occur so revisions must be drafted and submitted in a timely fashion. The group that meets to create new and/or refine existing selection criteria consists of various high level employees well versed in tax law from various organizations throughout the IRS. All proposed criteria undergo multiple levels of review to ensure consistent treatment and fairness in return selection.

In situations where computer scoring and selection does not occur, such as with Individual Taxpayer Identification Number (ITIN) referrals and amended returns, specific criteria are provided to Tax Examiners to be used in evaluating whether the item should be selected for examination or not. As with computer scoring, the information presented on the referral or the amended return must fall within the parameters defined in documented procedures for a selection to occur. It is also important to note that returns filed with a previously assigned ITIN are scored and considered for examination selection the same as any other return filed under a Social Security Number (SSN). The distinction is that returns filed by individuals who do not have an SSN, and have not previously been assigned an ITIN, must file those returns with Form W-7, *Application for IRS Individual Taxpayer Identification Number*. In addition to ensuring those returns are considered for examination potential, the Form W-7 and supporting documents must be reviewed as well. For the 2016 Filing Season, the IRS will be implementing the same automated rules-based selection criteria for returns filed with ITIN applications as it uses for any other return.

Moreover, fairness is embodied in the IRS's approach to taxpayer rights, a responsibility that we take seriously and that is a priority for all IRS employees in their work every day. Many of the rights in the TBOR, a cornerstone document that provides the nation's taxpayers with a better understanding of their rights, are aimed at ensuring that we discharge our mission with fairness and integrity (including, for example, the right to be informed, the right to finality, privacy and confidentiality). Further assurances of fairness and integrity within the selection and examination process are provided through administrative and legislative procedures. Prior to the assessment of any amount of additional tax or the reduction of a claimed refund, taxpayers are entitled to an administrative appeal before an Appeals Officer, who has not previously been involved with the case and, organizationally, is separate and independent of the function proposing the additional assessment. In addition to administrative safeguards, taxpayers may petition for a pre-assessment review of the proposed additional tax by the United States Tax Court. Consequently, we believe fairness and equitable treatment are already integral components of tax administration.

The IRS has clearly defined and documented program-level objectives, performance measures, indicators, and definitions of key concepts. The compliance program is supported by a robust set of measures that are key indicators of program performance. The mission of the Return Integrity and Compliance Services organization within W&I is to strengthen the integrity of the tax system by: protecting the public interest by improving IRS' ability to detect and prevent improper refunds; serving the public interest by taking actions fairly and appropriately to identify, evaluate and prevent the issuance of improper refunds; and, helping taxpayers understand the refundable tax credits for which they are eligible. Performance measures, such as the rate of audits resulting in no changes proposed to the reported tax, are indicative of the accuracy of the selection criteria in place and provide assurance of program integrity by validating that taxpayer and government resources are not being expended on the examination of substantially correct returns.

A response to your specific recommendations is enclosed. If you have any questions, please contact Ken Corbin, Director, Return Integrity and Compliance Services, Wage and Investment Division, at (404) 338-9042.

Sincerely,

John M. Dalrymple
Deputy Commissioner for
Services and Enforcement

Enclosure

Enclosure

To help ensure W&I meets its mission and selects audits fairly and with high integrity, we recommend that the Commissioner of Internal Revenue take the following seven actions:

Recommendation
Clearly define and document: 1) key terms such as "fairness"; and 2) W&I program level objectives, performance measures, and indicators for audit selection to evaluate whether the audit selection process is meeting its mission of applying the tax law with integrity and fairness to all.

Comment
We will review W&I program level objectives, performance measures and indicators to further ensure the audit selection process is meeting its mission of applying the tax law with integrity and fairness. The audit selection program is an autonomous process, evaluating and scoring each return under standard criteria, and without human intervention or bias. The objectives of the audit selection program are currently defined and are supported by a robust set of performance measures that, when considered in the context of the rules-based selection model, provide accurate indicators that program objectives are being met.

Recommendation
Clearly communicate these terms, objectives, measures, and indicators to all staff involved in the selection of returns for audit.

Comment
This will be communicated in written expectations at the beginning of each annual audit selection planning meeting.

Recommendation
Incorporate the new objectives(s) into W&I risk assessments done for audit selection processes.

Comment
If we find risks associated with the outlined expectations, we will follow the risk process to officially report them.

Recommendation
Ensure that internal control responsibilities are communicated and documented for all employees, including non-managers, tasked with revising or applying W&I audit selection criteria for potential audits.

Comment
Internal control information will be provided in the expectation document provided to each member of the annual audit selection planning meeting and receipt will be documented.

Recommendation
Develop and implement procedures to ensure that all criteria or methods used in programs to select returns for audit are consistently documented and approved.

Comment
Procedures are in place to document and approve the criteria and methods used in the return selection program. We will review these procedures to ensure all criteria or methods used are consistently documented and approved.

Recommendation
Develop and document a clear means for IRS staff members to promptly elevate to top management possible internal control issues related to audit selection in a timely manner.

Comment
We will expand existing feedback mechanisms to specifically cover the audit selection process.

Recommendation
Develop, document, and implement additional monitoring procedures to ensure audit selection controls and corrective actions are implemented in a timely manner.

Comment
We will review the processes that are in place for the documentation and timely implementation of selection controls and corrective actions to further ensure audit selection controls and corrective actions are implemented in a timely manner.

End Notes

[1] An audit—also referred to as an examination—is a review of a taxpayer's records that IRS conducts to determine whether income, expenses, credits, and other information are being reported accurately. Internal Revenue Code Sect. 6201 gives the Secretary of the Treasury, IRS's parent agency, the authority to conduct examinations.

[2] GAO, *IRS Examination Selection: Internal Controls for Exempt Organization Selection Should Be Strengthened,* GAO-15-514 (Washington, D.C.: July 13, 2015).

[3] GAO, *IRS Case Selection: Collection Process Is Largely Automated, but Lacks Adequate Internal Controls*, GAO-15-647 (Washington, D.C.: July 29, 2015), and *IRS Case Selection: Automated Collection System Lacks Key Internal Controls Needed to Ensure the Program Fulfills Its Mission*, GAO-15-744 (Washington: D.C.: Sept. 10, 2015).

[4] See GAO, *Internal Control Management and Evaluation Tool*, GAO-01-1008G (Washington, D.C.: Aug. 1, 2001), and *Standards for Internal Control in the Federal Government*, GAO/AIMD-00-21.3.1 (Washington, D.C.: November 1999).

[5] IRS, *Strategic Plan: FY2014-2017* (Washington, D.C.: 2014).

[6] To qualify, taxpayers must meet certain income and filing requirements and file a tax return, even if they do not owe any tax or are not required to file.

[7] An improper payment is defined by statute as any payment that should not have been made or that was made in an incorrect amount (including overpayments and underpayments) under statutory, contractual, administrative, or other legally applicable requirements. Among other things, it includes payment to an ineligible recipient, payment for an ineligible good or service, and any duplicate payment.

[8] GAO, *Improper Payments: Government-Wide Estimates and Use of Death Data to Help Prevent Payments to Deceased Individuals*, GAO-15-482T (Washington, D.C.: Mar. 16, 2015).

[9] 31 U.S.C. § 3321 note. Office of Management and Budget, Appendix C to Circular No. A-123, Requirements for Effective Estimation and Remediation of Improper Payments, OMB Memorandum M-15-02 (Washington, D.C.: Oct. 20, 2014); Financial Reporting Requirements - Revised, OMB Circular No. A-136 (Washington, D.C.: Sept. 18, 2014); and Protecting Privacy while Reducing Improper Payments with the Do Not Pay Initiative, OMB Memorandum M-13-20 (Washington, D.C.: Aug. 16, 2013).

[10] The Additional Child Tax Credit is available to certain individuals who get less than the full amount of the child tax credit and is refundable. 26 U.S.C. § 24(d). The American Opportunity Tax Credit is a refundable credit available to qualified taxpayers for postsecondary education. 26 U.S.C. § 25A(i). The Premium Tax Credit is a refundable credit that helps eligible individuals and families with low or moderate income afford health insurance purchased through a Health Insurance Marketplace. 26 U.S.C. § 36B

[11] SB/SE generally covers income taxes owed by self-employed individuals and small businesses with less than $10 million in assets as well as certain filers of employment, excise, estate, and gift tax returns.

[12] DDb is a system that uses a set of rules/criteria and scoring models along with internal and external data to evaluate tax returns to identify taxpayers who potentially do not meet eligibility requirements for the credit. This system scores returns daily and selects questionable returns for review/audit. The data include: 1) taxpayer data from IRS, 2) child custody information from the Department of Health and Human Services, 3) the dependent and child birth information from the Social Security Administration, and 4) prisoner information from the National Prisoner File to determine the validity of the claims on tax credits and refunds.

[13] Pub. L. No. 111-148, 124 Stat. 119 (Mar. 23, 2010), as amended by the Health Care and Education Reconciliation Act of 2010, Pub. L. No. 111-152,124 Stat.1029 (Mar. 30, 2010).

[14] The Business Modernization Office implements information technology solutions and re-engineered business processes.

[15] An ITIN is a nine-digit number issued by IRS to individuals who are required for U.S. tax purposes to have a U.S. taxpayer identification number but who do not have and are not eligible to get a Social Security number. IRS works ITIN cases to ensure that the numbers are issued in a timely manner to qualifying individuals and used for tax administration purposes.

[16] The term "revenue protection" refers to compliance activities that prevent refunds from being issued to taxpayers in the pre-refund environment. We have kept the statistics on recommended assessments and revenue protection separate to match IRS's publication on enforcement statistics.

[17] For the internal control standards, see GAO/AIMD-00-21.3.1. For a newer version of the standards, see GAO, *Standards for Internal Control in the Federal Government*, GAO-14-704G (Washington, D.C.: September 2014), which went into effect in fiscal year 2016. For

our review that started in October 2014, we used the November 1999 version. While the newer version has greater detail and depth, it retains the five components of internal control found in prior editions, which apply to all organizational levels and to all categories of objectives.

[18] For our review, we selected subfactors related to control environment from *Standards for Internal Control in the Federal Government* based on our preliminary work (e.g., review of various W&I workload templates that describe W&I's audit selection process). As noted earlier, the controls we chose applied to the processes and procedures that W&I officials described or for which they provided documentation regarding how audits were selected. While we relied on documentation demonstrating whether the standards were addressed, we did not test whether they were systemically applied.

[19] IRM is the primary, official source of "instructions to staff" on the administration and operation of IRS. It ensures that staff have the approved policy and guidance they need to carry out their responsibilities in administering tax laws or other agency obligations.

[20] IRM 6.735.1.

[21] IRS is required to use the fair and equitable treatment of taxpayers by employees as one of the standards for evaluating employee performance. Internal Revenue Service Restructuring and Reform Act of 1998, Pub. L. No. 105-206, § 1204(b), 112 Stat. 685, 722 (July 22, 1998) (IRS Restructuring and Reform Act of 1998).

[22] IRM 6.430.2.

[23] While we did not test how effectively IRS used the standard to rate staff, the Treasury Inspector General for Tax Administration (TIGTA) recently reported 26 instances in which 16 IRS managers did not maintain proper retention standard documentation that showed they evaluated their staff using the fair and equitable treatment of taxpayers as a performance standard. TIGTA, *Fiscal Year 2015 Statutory Audit of Compliance With Legal Guidelines Restricting the Use of Records of Tax Enforcement Results*, Reference Number: 2015-30-083 (Washington, D.C.: Sept. 16, 2015).

[24] Amended individual tax returns that include certain refundable tax credits may include the Additional Child Tax Credit, which is set aside for classification.

[25] According to IRS's fiscal years 2014-2017 Strategic Plan, IRS's mission is to "provide America's taxpayers top-quality service by helping them understand and meet their tax responsibilities and enforce the law with integrity and fairness to all." W&I's mission, as reflected in IRM 1.1.13.1, is "to provide its customers top quality service by helping them understand and comply with applicable tax laws and protect the public interest by applying the tax law with integrity and fairness to all."

[26] We reported in July and September 2015 that IRS has not clearly defined fairness and provided examples of differing explanations by IRS officials on how to achieve fairness in case selection. See GAO, *IRS Case Selection: Automated Collection System Lacks Key Internal Controls Needed to Ensure the Program Fulfills Its Mission*, GAO-15-744 (Washington, D.C.: Sept. 10, 2015); and *IRS Case Selection: Collection Process Is Largely Automated, but Lacks Adequate Internal Controls*, GAO-15-647 (Washington, D.C.: July 29, 2015).

[27] IRS's Strategic Plan for fiscal years 2014-2017 includes five other core values. They are: 1) respect, 2) continuous improvement, 3) inclusion, 4) openness and collaboration, and 5) personal accountability.

[28] IRM 4.19.10.

[29] W&I's operations plan contains activities that are intended to help implement goals contained in IRS's Strategic Plan. For example, the fiscal year 2016 operations plan has several activities on targeting high risk for noncompliance which links to IRS's strategic goal on effectively enforcing the law to ensure tax compliance and combating fraud.

[30] In our June 2014 report, we recommended that IRS document how decisions are to be made using performance information, but IRS did not mention whether it would document how all audit program significant decisions are to be made using performance information.

GAO, *IRS Correspondence Audits: Better Management Could Improve Tax Compliance and Reduce Taxpayer Burden*, GAO-14-479 (Washington, D.C.: June 5, 2014).

[31] See GAO-15-744 and GAO-15-647.

[32] We did not test how effectively IRS used the self-assessments to identify and address internal control deficiencies.

[33] Our work was not designed to test the effectiveness of access controls, including whether designated IT personnel had the appropriate access rights to modify W&I's audit selection criteria.

[34] Security authorization is the official management decision given by a senior organizational official to authorize operation of an information system and to explicitly accept the risk, which has been determined based on the testing of security controls.

[35] GAO, *Information Security: IRS Needs to Continue Improving Controls over Financial and Taxpayer Data*, GAO-15-337 (Washington, D.C.: Mar. 19, 2015).

[36] In its fiscal year 2015 Annual Audit Plan, TIGTA has an audit to determine whether IRS has implemented adequate security controls to address access, authentication, secure configuration, and logging on the mainframe operating systems within IRS's computing environment.

[37] IRM 2.127.2 specifies IT methods—such as unit, peer, and systems acceptability testing—to test whether software modifications are working as intended.

[38] IRM 1.4.2.11(5).

[39] IRM 1.1.13.

[40] GAO, *Standards for Internal Control in the Federal Government*, GAO-AIMD-00-21.3.1 (Washington, D.C.: November 1999).

[41] IRS, *Strategic Plan: FY2014-2017* (Washington, D.C.: 2014).

[42] GAO, *Internal Control Management and Evaluation Tool*, GAO-01-1008G (Washington, D.C.: August 2001).

In: IRS Audits
Editor: Kara Bradley

ISBN: 978-1-63485-724-6

Chapter 2

IRS RETURN SELECTION: CERTAIN INTERNAL CONTROLS FOR AUDITS IN THE SMALL BUSINESS AND SELF-EMPLOYED DIVISION SHOULD BE STRENGTHENED*

United States Government Accountability Office

WHY GAO DID THIS STUDY

IRS audits small businesses and self-employed individuals to ensure compliance with tax laws. Audits can help improve reporting compliance and reduce the tax gap—the difference between taxes owed and those voluntarily paid on time, which is estimated at $385 billion annually after late payments and enforcement actions. Therefore, it is important that IRS makes informed decisions about how it selects taxpayers for audit.

GAO was asked to review IRS's processes and controls for selecting Small Business/Self-Employed (SB/SE) taxpayers for audit. This report (1) describes these processes and (2) determines how well SB/SE's selection processes and controls support its mission to apply the tax law with integrity and fairness to all.

---

* This is an edited, reformatted and augmented version of the United States Government Accountability Office publication, GAO-16-103, dated December 2015.

GAO reviewed IRS criteria, processes, and control procedures for selecting taxpayers for audit; assessed whether IRS control procedures followed *Standards for Internal Control in the Federal Government*; and reviewed nonprobability samples of over 200 audit files. GAO also conducted eight focus groups with SB/SE staff who review or make audit selection decisions and interviewed IRS officials.

WHAT GAO RECOMMENDS

GAO recommends that IRS take seven actions to help ensure that the audit selection program meets its mission, such as establishing and communicating program objectives related to audit selection and improving procedures for documenting and monitoring the selection process. In commenting on a draft of this report, IRS agreed with the recommendations.

WHAT GAO FOUND

The Small Business/Self-Employed (SB/SE) division of the Internal Revenue Service (IRS) uses over 30 methods, called workstreams, to identify and review tax returns that may merit an audit. These returns were initially identified through seven sources which include referrals; computer programs that run filters, rules, or algorithms to identify potentially noncompliant taxpayers; and related returns that are identified in the course of another audit.

SB/SE's workstreams follow a general, multiphase process for identifying, reviewing (classifying), and selecting returns for audit. Within this general approach, the selection process varies across workstreams. Differences include the number of review steps and manual processes, which are greater for field audits compared to correspondence audits which generally focus on a single compliance issue and are identified using automated processes. For fiscal year 2013, IRS reported that SB/SE's primary workstream for field audits identified about 1.6 million returns as potentially most noncompliant. About 77,500 returns (5 percent) were selected for audit, a much smaller pool of returns than was initially identified.

SB/SE has control procedures for safeguarding data and segregating duties across the overall selection process, among others, but it has not implemented other key internal controls. The lack of strong control procedures increases the risk that the audit program's mission of fair and equitable application of the tax laws will not be achieved. Examples of internal control deficiencies include the following:

Program objectives and key term of fairness are not clearly defined. Fairness is specified in SB/SE's mission statement and referenced in IRS's procedures for auditors. However, IRS has not defined fairness or program objectives for audit selection that would support its mission of treating taxpayers fairly. GAO heard different interpretations of fairness from focus group participants. Not having a clear definition of fairness can unintentionally lead to inconsistent treatment of taxpayers and create doubts as to how fairly IRS administers the tax law. Further, the lack of clearly articulated objectives undercuts the effectiveness of SB/SE's efforts to assess risks and measure performance toward achieving these objectives.

Procedures for documenting and monitoring selection decisions are not consistent. SB/SE does not always require selection decisions and rationales to be documented. For example, SB/SE requires that some workstreams document survey decisions (when returns are not assigned for audit), rationale, and approval using a form. Other workstreams, such as its primary workstream for field audits, require a group manager stamp but do not require the rationale to be documented. Also, SB/SE does not always require classification decisions (when returns are assessed for audit potential and compliance issues) to be reviewed. Having procedures to ensure that selection decisions and rationale are consistently documented and reviewed can reduce the potential for error and unfairness.

ABBREVIATIONS

AIMS	Audit Information Management System
ASFR	Automated Substitute for Return
AUR	Automated Underreporter
CIP	Compliance Initiative Project
CRC	Campus Reporting Compliance
DDb	Dependent Database
DEBR	Discretionary Exam Business Rules
DIF	Discriminant Function
E&G	Estate and Gift
EITC	Earned Income Tax Credit

ERM	Enterprise Risk Management
GLD	Government Liaison and Disclosure
IRM	Internal Revenue Manual
IRS	Internal Revenue Service
NRP	National Research Program
SARP	State Audit Referral Program
SB/SE	Small Business/Self-Employed Division
SFR	Substitute for Return
TEFRA	Tax Equity and Fiscal Responsibility Act of 1982
TIGTA	Treasury Inspector General for Tax Administration
W&I	Wage and Investment

***

December 16, 2015

The Honorable Kevin Brady
Chairman
Committee on Ways and Means
House of Representatives

The Honorable Peter Roskam
Chairman
Subcommittee on Oversight
Committee on Ways and Means
House of Representatives

The Internal Revenue Service's (IRS) Small Business/Self-Employed Division (SB/SE)—one of four IRS operating divisions—oversees about 57 million taxpayers who file income, employment, excise, estate, or gift returns.[1] SB/SE's enforcement responsibilities include auditing individual and business tax returns to detect misreporting.[2] Audits can help improve reporting compliance and reduce the tax gap—the difference between taxes owed and those paid voluntarily and on time.[3] As we have previously reported, small businesses are a key contributor to the tax gap.[4] Nearly 40 percent, or $179 billion, of the tax gap can be attributed to the underreporting of both business income on individual income tax returns and the self-employment tax that is largely assessed on business income for self-employed taxpayers. An additional 4 percent of the tax gap, or $19 billion, can be attributed to underreporting by small corporations, which IRS defines as having less than $10 million in assets.

Audits provide IRS with an important enforcement tool to identify noncompliance in reporting tax obligations as well as to enhance voluntary reporting compliance. If taxpayers perceive the selection of returns for audit as unfair, their confidence in IRS could be undermined and voluntary compliance could be undercut. The mission of IRS, as well as SB/SE, incorporates these concepts of ensuring compliance and fairly applying the tax law.[5]

Given the concerns expressed about the fairness of selecting taxpayers for review, you asked us to review SB/SE's processes and controls for selecting returns for audit.[6] This report (1) describes SB/SE's processes for selecting returns for audit; and (2) assesses how well SB/SE's processes and controls for selecting returns for audit support its mission, including applying the tax law with integrity and fairness to all

For the first objective, we reviewed IRS documents to understand the processes and procedures that SB/SE uses to prioritize, identify, review, and select returns for audit, as well as how SB/SE documents selection decisions. For the second objective, we reviewed the procedures identified above that SB/SE uses to help achieve its stated mission of applying "the tax law with integrity and fairness to all." We then assessed whether these procedures adhered to relevant federal standards for internal controls.[7] To determine the extent to which SB/SE implemented its selection procedures, we conducted a file review consisting of (1) a nongeneralizable sample of 173 SB/SE audit cases opened between March 2014 and February 2015, (2) a nongeneralizable sample of 30 evaluations on how well SB/SE staff reviewed returns, and (3) a nongeneralizable sample of 30 returns that were selected for audit but later removed, or screened out, from the audit inventory (i.e., surveyed).[8] While our samples are not representative of their populations, we selected the samples to ensure coverage across a broad range of key criteria and dimensions, including the extent to which manual processes are involved. We used the results of the file review in combination with other sources of information to assess the internal controls that help safeguard the fairness of the return selection process, and not to specifically look for cases of inappropriate selection. We also conducted eight focus groups with selected SB/SE staff who are responsible for reviewing or making return selection decisions. For both objectives, we analyzed data from IRS's Audit Information Management System. Based on our testing of the data and review of documentation and interviews, we determined that these data were reliable for the purposes of this report. Finally, we interviewed SB/SE officials about return selection processes and procedures, and to discuss any potential deficiencies we identified.

We conducted this performance audit from September 2014 to December 2015 in accordance with generally accepted government auditing standards. Those standards require that we plan and perform the audit to obtain sufficient, appropriate evidence to provide a reasonable basis for our findings and conclusions based on our audit objectives. We believe that the evidence obtained provides a reasonable basis for our findings and conclusions based on our audit objectives. More detailed information on our scope and methodology appears in appendix I.

BACKGROUND

IRS's operating divisions develop annual plans to guide audit decisions in terms of the number of returns to be audited. SB/SE audit plans strive to balance the number of audits in any fiscal year across all types of tax returns (e.g., individual income tax returns) and taxpayers (e.g., individual wage earners, small businesses, corporations) given the available number and location of IRS auditors, and knowledge about types of noncompliance to pursue through audits.

SB/SE conducts audits through field offices located in seven regional areas. These audits generally are conducted by meeting with the taxpayer and/or his or her representatives. The field auditors include revenue agents who tend to audit the most complex returns and tax compliance officers who tend to audit simpler returns. SB/SE also does audits through its four campus locations; these audits tend to be the simplest and are generally done by tax examiners through correspondence with the taxpayers.[9] Figure 1 shows an organizational chart of IRS's operating divisions and SB/SE's audit offices.

In fiscal year 2014, SB/SE closed 823,904 audits, representing more than half of nearly 1.4 million closed audits across IRS in fiscal year 2014. SB/SE audits resulted in over $12 billion of the $33 billion in total recommended additional taxes across all IRS audits.[10] For details on results of SB/SE audits, see appendix II.

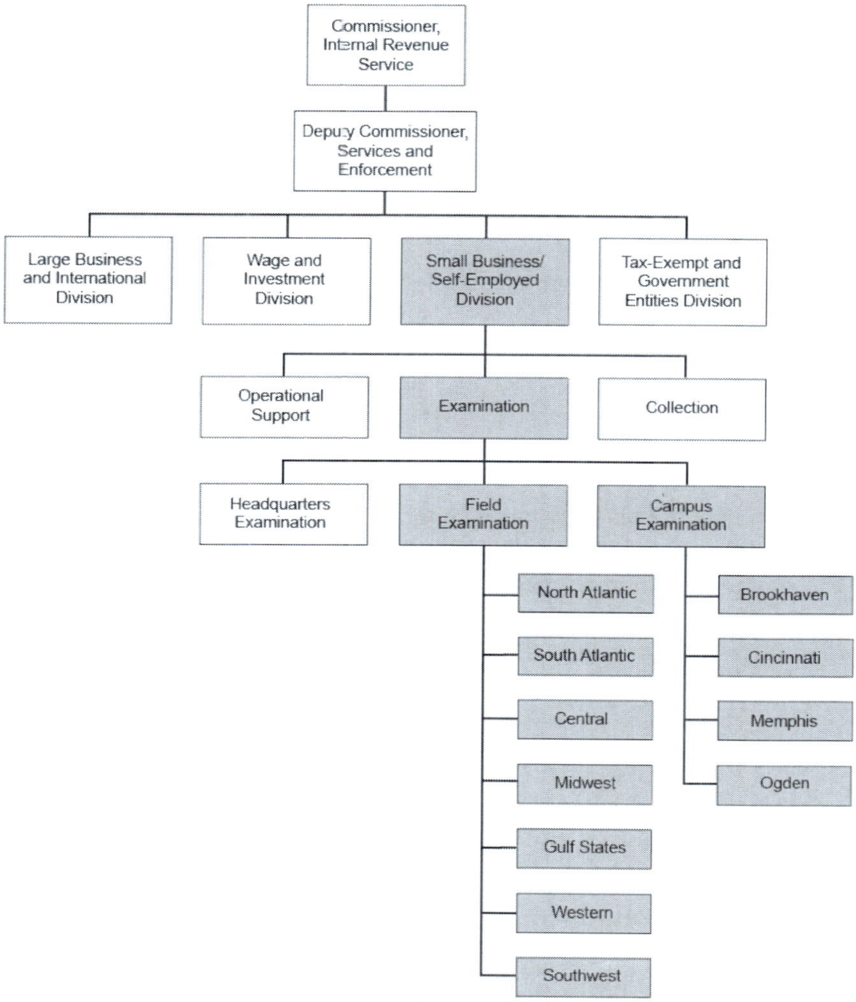

Source: GAO analysis of IRS information. | GAO-16-103.

Figure 1. Organizational Chart of IRS Operating Divisions and SB/SE Audit Offices.

In addition to audits, IRS conducts nonaudit compliance checks, which may lead to an audit. These checks include the Math Error, Automated Underreporter (AUR), and Automated Substitute for Return (ASFR) programs. The Math Error program electronically reviews tax returns as they are filed for basic computational errors or missing forms/schedules. Several months after returns have been filed, AUR electronically matches information reported by third parties, such as banks or employers, against the information that taxpayers report on their tax returns. This matching helps identify potentially underreported income or unwarranted deductions or tax credits. ASFR also uses information return data to identify persons who did not file returns; constructs substitute tax returns for certain nonfilers; and assesses tax, interest, and penalties based on those substitute returns. Although these and other compliance checks may identify potentially noncompliant tax returns that are subsequently audited, these programs are not the subject of this report.

In March 2014, IRS's Chief Risk Officer, who oversees its agency-wide program to identify and assess risks, completed a high-level, risk-based review of the IRS audit selection process.[11] The review focused on the potential for bias based on the judgment of the Risk Officer and not on analysis against objective standards, such as comparing steps in the process to the internal control standards. Even so, the Risk Officer concluded that IRS maintained sound internal controls in its audit programs and that the risk of partiality in IRS's audit selection was very low. The risk of partiality appeared lowest in the automated selection programs. It appeared to be slightly higher for manual selection and referral programs because greater employee judgment was involved.

SB/SE Uses a Multiphase Process and Many Methods to Identify and Review Returns for Potential Audit; Most Returns Are Not Selected

SB/SE Uses a Multiphase Process to Select Tax Returns for Audit

SB/SE selects potentially noncompliant tax returns for audit using a multiphase process intended to enable IRS to narrow the large pool of available returns to those that most merit investment of audit resources. As shown in figure 2, in broad terms, this process generally includes (1) identifying an initial inventory of tax returns that have audit potential (e.g., reporting noncompliance), (2) reviewing that audit potential to reduce the number of returns that merit selection for audit (termed "classification"), (3) selecting returns by assigning them to auditors based on a field manager's review of audit potential given available resources and needs, and (4) auditing selected returns.[12]

SB/SE Uses More Than 30 Methods to Identify and Review Returns for Potential Audit

SB/SE uses 33 methods, called workstreams, to identify and review tax returns that may merit an audit.[13] These workstreams can be categorized into seven groups based on how the return was initially identified (see appendix IV for a table of workstreams by group).[14] We have listed these groups in general order of how much discretion is involved in identifying, reviewing, and selecting returns, starting with those that involve more discretion. This ordering does not correspond to the number of audits conducted. For example, although referrals generally involve more discretion in selecting returns for audit, they do not make up the largest percentage of SB/SE field audits (see figure 3).

- **Referrals.** IRS employees and units, as well as external sources, such as other agencies and citizens, can refer potentially noncompliant taxpayers to SB/SE. SB/SE may start an audit if the referral indicates significant potential for noncompliance. Referrals can involve, among others, those promoting shelters created to avoid taxation, whistleblowers, and those not filing required tax returns.[15]
- **Related pickups.** After opening an audit, SB/SE may identify the taxpayer's prior or subsequent year returns or returns of related taxpayers to audit.
- **User-developed criteria.** These criteria use filters or rules embedded in computer software to identify returns with specific characteristics, often for projects. These characteristics generally involve a specific tax issue known or suspected to have high noncompliance in a particular geographic area, industry, or population. For example, the criteria may be used for projects that explore or test ways to uncover noncompliance or improve compliance.
- **Computer programs.** Computer programs use rules or formulas to identify potential noncompliance across a type of tax return, rather than for a specific tax issue. For example, IRS uses a computer algorithm, the discriminant function (DIF), to determine the probability of noncompliance somewhere on the tax return. When a

return receives a high enough score, SB/SE may review the return for audit potential.

- **Data matching.** When information on a tax return—such as wages, interest, and dividends—does not match information provided to IRS by states, employers, or other third parties, these discrepancies may prompt SB/SE to review returns for audit potential. An example of a workstream that uses data matching is the payment card income pilot, which uses information from credit card transactions to identify income that may be underreported.[16]
- **Taxpayer-initiated.** When taxpayers contact IRS to request an adjustment to their respective tax returns, tax refunds, or tax credits, or request to have a previous audit reconsidered, SB/SE may initiate an audit after reviewing these requests.
- **Random identification.** The National Research Program (NRP) studies tax compliance through audits of a randomly-identified sample of tax returns.[17] Specifically, NRP measures voluntary compliance in reporting income, deductions, and credits, among other categories, and generalizes those measures to the population being studied.

SB/SE Selection Methods Have Similarities but Also Vary

All of SB/SE's selection methods or workstreams follow the general multiphase selection process to identify and review potentially noncompliant returns before selecting and actually auditing them. Workstreams also share some common characteristics. For example, multiple staff are involved in the various phases so that one person cannot control the entire process. About one-third of the workstreams use some form of automation to identify the returns that should enter the workstream. Most workstreams involve some form of manual review to determine which returns have audit potential. For example, IRS auditors review (i.e., classify) tax returns identified as having audit potential to determine which returns have the highest potential and which parts of the return should be audited. Finally, all workstreams screen out returns as part of the review process.[18] This winnowing means that the large pool of returns initially identified as having audit potential becomes a much smaller pool of returns that are selected for audit.

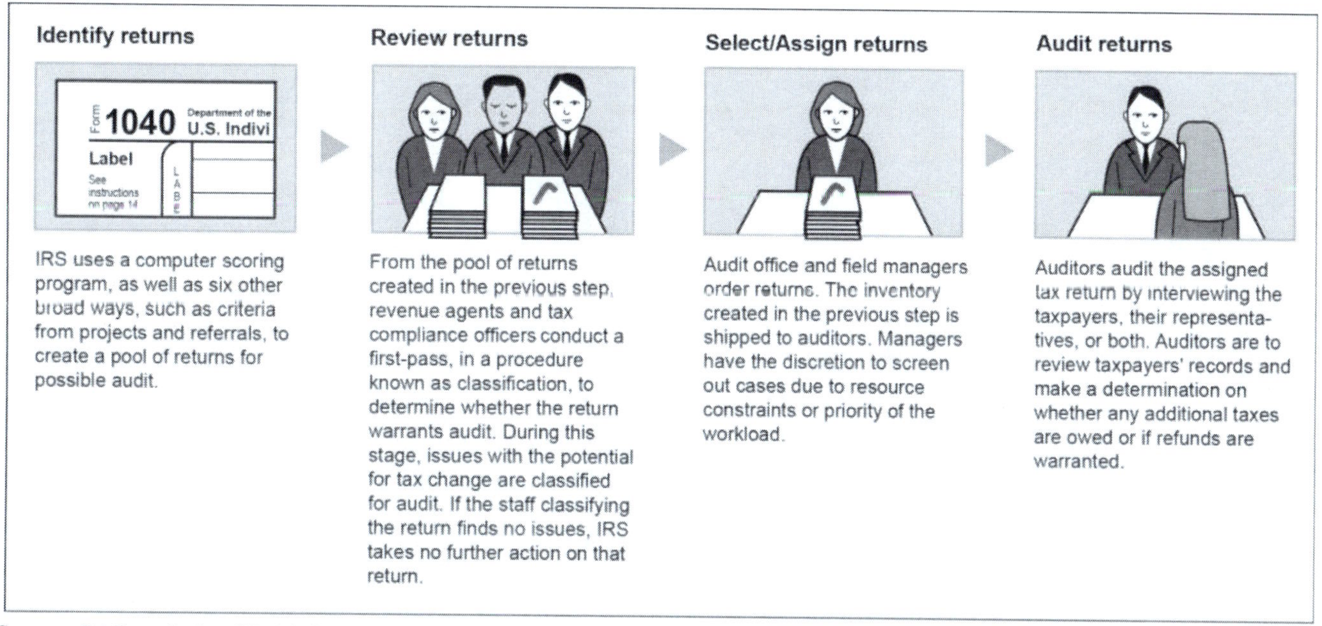

Source: GAO analysis of IRS information. | GAO-16-103

Figure 2. SB/SE's General Process for Selecting Returns for Audit.

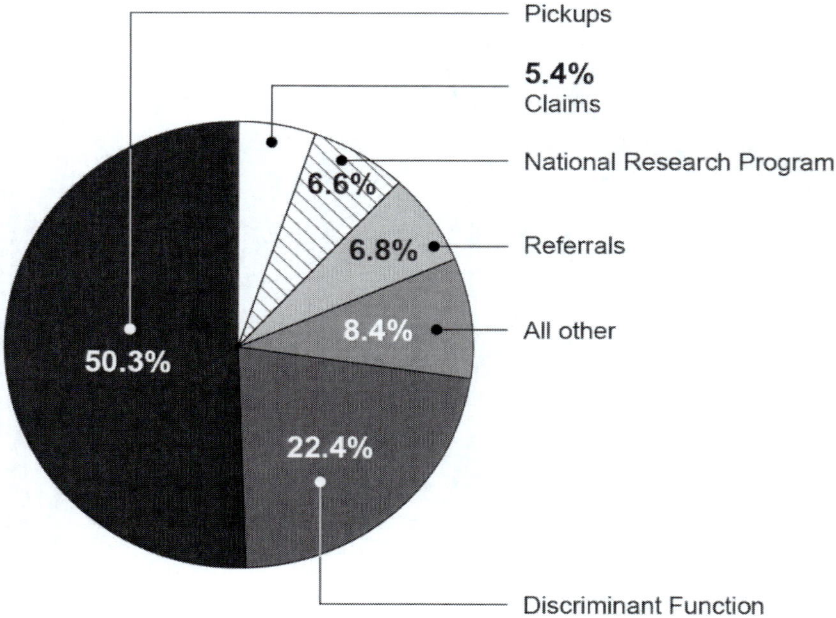

Source: GAO analysis of IRS information. | GAO-16-103

Notes: Referrals include internal sources such as tax shelter audits and external sources such as state referrals or information reports provided by taxpayers. Claims include requests for refunds or reduction of tax liabilities assessed. All other includes several workstreams that each accounted for less than 3 percent of total SB/SE field audit closed cases in fiscal year 2014.

Figure 3. Percent of SB/SE Closed Field Audits by Workstream or Identification Group, Fiscal Year 2014.

However, variations exist among the workstreams, particularly between the field and campus. For example, the field process generally uses more review steps and manual involvement (e.g., classification) than for campus. The latter generally focuses on a single compliance issue and relies more on automated filters and rules to identify returns. Among field workstreams, the extent of review varies. For example, a few workstreams use a committee to review proposals and authorize new projects or investigations before returns can enter the workstream. Also, for field audits, group managers generally decide whether to assign, hold, or screen out returns for audit, whereas returns selected for campus audits are generally assigned through automated processes after campus analysts review the returns to ensure that they adhere to the selection rules embedded in the automated processes. Some workstreams, such as taxpayer claims and some referrals, involve more manual processes to identify and review returns; other workstreams involve both manual and automated processes or are almost entirely automated. Finally, the procedures for screening out returns vary across workstreams.[19]

SB/SE Relied on Different Methods in Its Field and Campus Locations to Select Most Returns for Audit

In fiscal year 2014, related pickups from various identification methods or workstreams accounted for about 50 percent of SB/SE closed field audits.[20] Most of these pickups were related to various ways in which taxpayers attempt to shelter income from taxation and DIF-sourced returns. The DIF workstream alone (part of the computer program identification group) accounted for over 22 percent of SB/SE closed field audits, and various referral workstreams accounted for nearly 7 percent, as shown in figure 3. For details on the workstreams included in the categories shown in figure 3, see appendix VI.

For campus audits closed in fiscal year 2014, available IRS data showed that 31 percent focused on the Earned Income Tax Credit (EITC).[21] SB/SE relies on a computer program known as the Dependent Database (DDb) to identify most of the returns to be audited for EITC issues. DDb is a rules-based system that identifies potential noncompliance related to tax benefits based on the dependency and residency of children. According to IRS, DDb rules are reviewed yearly for changes, and no additional filtering or review is needed on the cases that are selected for audit. In fiscal year 2014, DDb identified more than 77 percent of the closed EITC audits. The other approximate 23 percent of closed EITC audits were identified using various other methods, such as referrals from within IRS and pickups related to audits of other tax returns.

Most Returns SB/SE Identified for Potential Audit Were Not Selected

SB/SE does not have complete data on the number of returns that are initially identified as having audit potential, reviewed, and selected for audit for all 33 workstreams. Using data that are available, table 1 illustrates differences in the extent to which returns are winnowed from identification through selection for two workstreams. For example, about half of the DIF-sourced returns reviewed were selected for audit, and almost all returns reviewed for NRP were selected for audit.[22]

Some SB/SE Procedures for Selecting Returns for Audit Met Internal Control Standards, but Objectives Were Unclear and Documentation and Monitoring Procedures Were Inconsistent

An effective internal control system can help federal agencies achieve their missions and objectives and improve accountability. As set forth in *Standards for Internal Control in the Federal Government*, also known as the Green Book, internal controls comprise the plans, methods, and procedures used to meet an entity's mission, goals, and objectives, which support performance-based management.[23] Internal controls help agency program managers achieve desired results. They also provide reasonable assurance that program objectives are being achieved through, among other things, effective and efficient use of resources. Internal control is not one event, but rather a series of actions and activities that occur throughout an entity's operations and on an ongoing basis. Two examples of internal control standards are the establishment of clearly defined objectives and a commitment to documenting significant events.

SB/SE has some procedures in place that are consistent with internal control standards. However, we identified some internal control weaknesses that leave SB/SE vulnerable to inconsistent return selection for audit or the perception of it.

Some SB/SE Procedures Met Internal Control Standards

Our review of IRS and SB/SE procedures on selecting returns for audit found several procedures that adhered to internal control standards which provided some assurance of fairness and integrity in the selection process.[24] For our review, we relied on documentation demonstrating that the standards were employed and did not independently test whether the standards were systemically applied.[25]

Table 1. Number of Returns Identified, Reviewed, and Selected for Field Audit for DIF and NRP Workstreams, Fiscal Year 2013

	Fiscal Year 2013			
Selection workstream	**Returns identified for potential audit**	**Returns reviewed**	**Returns sent for assignment**	**Returns selected for audit**
DIF	1,552,714[a]	151,836	138,886	77,446
NRP	144,874,882[b]	14,687	13,870	13,449

Source: IRS. | GAO-16-103

Notes: We used fiscal year 2013 to allow more time for audit return selection, which can occur for up to 3 years after returns are filed and because complete data for 2014 was not available at the time of our review. Estimated numbers only include field audits and primary returns. NRP returns are reported by tax year, not fiscal year.

[a] This is the number of individual tax returns filed whose DIF score exceeded the threshold for determining which returns were potentially most noncompliant.

[b] This is the number of all Form 1040 individual income tax returns filed, which are eligible for random selection under NRP. Randomly selecting returns enables IRS to generalize estimates of reporting compliance to the population of all such returns filed.

- **Ethics.** SB/SE demonstrated a commitment to promoting ethical behavior among staff, which provides some high-level assurance that it may be able to meet its goal of integrity and fair treatment of taxpayers in general. For example, IRS's ethics training and annual certification process provide some assurance that IRS staff should be aware of the need to act ethically and impartially.
- **Awareness of internal controls by managers.** SB/SE has demonstrated a commitment to employ internal control activities to ensure accountability in achieving its mission. All managers are required to do an annual self-assessment of internal control procedures. To the extent that SB/SE managers report deficiencies and SB/SE uses the results, the annual self-assessment can provide assurance that the importance of internal control is understood in SB/SE. Our work was not designed to test how effectively IRS used the self-assessments to identify and address deficiencies.
- **Segregation of duties.** All of SB/SE's selection workstreams involve multiple parties so that no individual can control the decision-making process. For example, staff who classify a return cannot later audit the

same return. Also, for field audits, IRS coordinators in an area office generally determine which returns will be assigned to the field offices, rather than field offices and auditors generating their own work. SB/SE also has procedures to ensure that managers review about 10 percent of returns classified for the DIF and NRP workstreams. Also, managers must approve auditors' requests to open audits for prior or subsequent year and related returns. Although not every step in the selection process is reviewed, these procedures provide some assurance that the decision to audit a return is not determined unilaterally.

- **Safeguarding data/systems.** SB/SE demonstrated that safeguards are in place to restrict system access to authorized users. IRS has procedures on system security and uses a multitiered authentication process to control system access, which we observed.

SB/SE Has Not Clearly Defined or Communicated "Fairness" in Its Return Selection Process

The mission statements for both IRS and SB/SE declare the strategic goal of administering the "tax law with integrity and fairness to all." SB/SE officials stated that integrity and fairness are core values of IRS. However, they did not define these terms or provide evidence that staff know what is to be achieved by this strategic goal. Without a clear definition of fairness that has been communicated to staff, SB/SE has less assurance that its staff consistently treat all taxpayers fairly.

INTERNAL CONTROL STANDARD: DEFINE OBJECTIVES

Internal control standards call for program objectives to be clearly defined in measurable terms to enable the design of internal control for related risks. Specific terms should be fully defined and clearly set forth so they can be easily understood at all levels of the entity. Consistent information must be reliably communicated throughout the entity if the entity is to achieve its goals.

Source: GAO. | GAO-16-103.

IRS's procedures manual, the Internal Revenue Manual (IRM), references behaviors auditors are to follow related to fairness, which may promote taxpayer confidence in IRS.[26] For example,

> "The purpose of the Internal Revenue Service is to collect the proper amount of tax revenues at the least cost to the public, and in a manner that warrants the highest degree of public confidence in our integrity, efficiency and fairness."
>
> "All [auditors] must perform their professional responsibilities in a way that supports the IRS Mission. This requires auditors to provide top quality service and to apply the law with integrity and fairness to all."
>
> "The obligation to protect taxpayer privacy and to safeguard the information taxpayers entrust to us is a fundamental part of the Service's mission to apply the tax law with integrity and fairness to all."
>
> "Requirements governing the accuracy, reliability, completeness, and timeliness of taxpayer information will be such as to ensure fair treatment of all taxpayers."

These references point to the overall concept of fairness without explaining what it means, particularly when selecting tax returns for audit. Fairness can be difficult to define because everyone may have different concepts of what constitutes fair treatment. We heard different interpretations of fairness and integrity from IRS participants involved in the selection process during the eight focus groups we conducted. Given the different interpretations, not having a clear definition of fairness unintentionally can lead to inconsistent treatment of taxpayers and create doubts as to how fairly IRS administers the tax law. In our focus groups, SB/SE staff stated that they viewed audit selection as fair when they:

- focus on large, unusual, and questionable items,
- do not consider taxpayer's name, location, etc.,
- avoid auditing taxpayers they know or may be in their neighborhood,
- treat issues consistently across returns,
- apply same standards,
- treat all taxpayers the same,
- account for varying costs across locations (e.g., housing costs), and
- avoid being influenced by personal preferences.

Each comment represents someone's concept of fairness. According to SB/SE officials, IRS relies on the judgment of its staff to determine what is fair. Although many concepts sound similar, they can be different, or even incompatible. For example, some participants said that not considering a taxpayer's name or geographic location was fair treatment. However, other participants said that considering geographic location was necessary to avoid auditing taxpayers they knew or to determine whether expenses were reasonable for that location (e.g., larger expenses may be reasonable for high-cost locations). Also, some audit projects focus on indications of certain types of noncompliance in specific locations, such as an IRS area or a state. SB/SE officials stated that both views of fairness regarding location may be appropriate for classification.

We reviewed training materials used to instruct revenue agents in the decision-making process when selecting returns to audit, as well as the orientation briefing provided to staff assigned to classification details.[27] Our review of the documentation, as well as discussions with focus group participants involved in classification, indicate that the training materials and the briefing have not defined fairness or how to apply it consistently when selecting returns for audit.[28]

Another challenge to treating all taxpayers consistently or under the same standard arises when the group manager in the field has to manage resource constraints. Some group managers talked about not having the right type and grade of auditor in a location to select a particular return that was deemed worth auditing. Others talked about not having enough travel money for auditors to justify selecting some tax returns. Group managers in other locations may be able to select a similar return because they have fewer of these constraints.

In addition, SB/SE officials said that what is fair may vary depending on the role of the IRS staff involved. They said IRS staff members may have different perspectives of what is "fair" depending on their responsibilities and position, such as IRS staff who are analysts or managers in headquarters versus analysts, auditors, and their managers in the field.

SB/SE Has Not Established Objectives for Fair Selection of Returns for Audit, Which Challenges Performance Measurement and Risk Management

SB/SE has not established objectives on the fair selection of returns. Without a definition of fairness, SB/SE cannot be assured that an objective for fair selection clearly indicates what is to be achieved. For example, objectives could be based on definitions of fairness that we heard in our focus groups, such as the extent to which selection occurs because of large, unusual, and questionable items on a return or because SB/SE is applying the same standards to similar tax returns.

INTERNAL CONTROL STANDARD: ASSESS RISKS AND PERFORMANCE TO OBJECTIVES

Internal control standards call for management to set program objectives that align with an entity's mission, strategic plan, goals, and applicable laws and regulations. Clearly-defined objectives can enhance the effectiveness and efficiency of a program's operations and are necessary to assess risks. Objectives should clearly define what is to be achieved, who is to achieve it, and how and when it will be achieved. Documenting objectives promotes consistent understanding.

Source: GAO. | GAO-16-103.

SB/SE develops audit objectives in its annual work plan. For fiscal year 2014, audit objectives included (1) review workload identification and selection models, collaborate with other IRS units to revise processes/guidelines, and develop guidance and monitoring tools to ensure consistent application; and (2) use more research data to develop alternative workload identification streams and delivery. These objectives address the process of selecting returns but not whether returns are selected fairly. For example, applying selection models and processes consistently does not ensure that the models and processes were designed to achieve fairness. Further, IRS has not identified a level of consistency that would indicate that fairness has been achieved.[29]

Without clearly-defined objectives aligned to its mission and a clear understanding across SB/SE of how fairness is defined, SB/SE has less assurance that it is measuring progress toward or achieving its strategic goal of treating taxpayers fairly.

IRS Has Established Performance Measures, but None Directly Assessing Fair Selection of Returns for Audit

Given that SB/SE does not have clearly-defined objectives on fair selection, it also does not have performance measures aligned with these objectives and explicitly tied to integrity or fairness. For example, if IRS defined fairness as focusing on large, unusual, and questionable items and developed an objective based on this definition, performance measures could assess the quality and extent to which auditors focused on these items. SB/SE officials pointed to a variety of existing performance measures that they believe assess whether selection processes were impartial and consistent. Examples of these performance measures include:

- IRS's Customer Satisfaction survey asks taxpayers to rate their satisfaction with the auditor's explanation for how the return was selected for audit.[30] However, SB/SE did not show how answers were used to assess whether the selection process was fair or modify the process to make it fair. Further, taxpayer dissatisfaction is subjective, and taxpayers would not have context to know why their returns were selected compared to others.
- SB/SE conducts business reviews to assess how well its selection process is performing. However, concerns raised in these reviews focused on selection process steps, such as ordering returns and conducting research projects, instead of the underlying fairness of selecting a return.
- All employees are to be evaluated on how well they provide fair and equitable treatment to taxpayers as required by the Internal Revenue Service Restructuring and Reform Act of 1998; the IRM provides examples of behaviors that would meet this requirement.[31] These behaviors may be consistent with IRS's mission, but they focus on how taxpayers were treated after the audit started rather than how auditors reviewed returns for potential audit selection.

Without performance measures that align with objectives to achieve fair selection, SB/SE lacks assurance that it can measure progress toward fair return selection.

IRS Has Taken Steps to Identify Risks, but Linkage to Audit Selection Objectives Is Needed

IRS's efforts to identify risks and assess whether and how to manage them operate under two complementary approaches.

- **Internal controls framework.** The procedures in IRM 1.4.2 govern IRS's processes for monitoring and improving internal controls, which include the identification and mitigation of risks. Managers are expected to understand the risks associated with their operations and ensure that controls are in place and operating properly to mitigate those risks.
- **Enterprise Risk Management (ERM).** ERM is broader in scope than internal controls, focusing on agency-wide risks. ERM is intended to help organizations in setting strategy to consider risk and how much risk the organization is willing to accept. IRS implemented ERM in February 2014 to increase awareness by IRS management of IRS- wide risks and to serve as an early-warning system to identify emerging challenges and address them before they affect operations.[32]

Both approaches to risk management require clear, defined objectives in measurable terms to identify and analyze risks that could challenge achieving desired outcomes. Risks toward achieving those objectives can be identified and analyzed, and risk tolerances can be determined.[33] Understanding the significance of the risks to achieving objectives provides the basis for responding to the risks.

Without clear audit selection objectives on fairness, SB/SE lacks assurance that it can identify and assess risks to the fair selection of returns to audit. Absent risk identification and assessments linked to program objectives, vulnerabilities may go unaddressed, which could lead to unfair return selection.

SB/SE Has Not Consistently Documented Audit Selection Procedures and Decisions

We found many instances where SB/SE documented the review and selection of returns for audit. However, we also found several instances where SB/SE did not document various aspects of its return selection process nor locate documentation in time for our review.

INTERNAL CONTROL STANDARD: DOCUMENT TRANSACTIONS

Internal control and all transactions and other significant events need to be clearly documented, and the documentation should be readily available for review.

Source: GAO. | GAO-16-103

- **Audit plan changes.** Changes to the field audit plan are documented during the annual planning process, but SB/SE did not document its process for modifying the field audit plan during the year. According to SB/SE officials, they modify the plan during the year as additional budget and staffing information from IRS's finance unit becomes available. Officials stated that changes to this audit plan are documented by the budget information received and by the recalculated plan. However, SB/SE did not document how it translated the budget and staffing information into changes in the inventory targets or staffing nor why some targets were changed but not others.
- **Selection decisions and rationale.** SB/SE did not consistently document decisions for selecting certain tax returns over others for audit and the rationale behind the decisions. SB/SE does not require all of these decisions and rationales to be documented. Returns that are stored electronically and are deemed to be excess inventory can be screened out without documentation such as a form, stamp, or signature. For discriminant function (DIF)-sourced returns, SB/SE's primary workstream for field audits, and some referrals, only a group manager stamp is required to screen out the returns, rather than also documenting the rationale for screening them out.[34] Documentation requirements also vary within a workstream. For example, for returns involving a tax shelter fostered by a promoter, audit screen-out rationales are required to be documented at the group level in the field but not at the area office level. Officials said that, aside from the Form 1900 for certain returns, they generally do not document why a return was not selected. To illustrate, we found nine files without documentation of the screen-out decision or rationale in our file

review of 30 screened-out returns.[35] Regardless of whether a form is required, the screen-out decision should be documented.

- **Files not located.** IRS could not locate 18 of the 233 files we requested in time for our review.[36] For example, for non-DIF pickup returns, 5 out of 24 files requested were not located in time. For all types of referrals we reviewed, we were unable to review 8 out of 56 files requested because they were not located in time. According to officials, IRS could not locate these files because files for one audit may be stored with files for any number of related audits, files for open or recently closed audits may not yet be available, and files may have been stored in the wrong location.

In addition to internal control standards, the IRM requires all records to be efficiently managed until final disposition.[37]

Having procedures to ensure that selection decisions and rationale are clearly and consistently documented helps provide assurance that management directives are consistently followed and return selection decisions are made fairly. Further, being able to find files efficiently can aid congressional and other oversight, and prevent unnecessary taxpayer burden if IRS later needs to contact the taxpayer regarding material that would have been in the file.

SB/SE Has Not Regularly Monitored Decisions Made and Coding Used for Audit Selection

As discussed earlier in this report, SB/SE has procedures that, if implemented, help provide some assurance that its return selection process is generally monitored. However, we found that SB/SE did not have requirements to monitor certain steps in the selection process.

- **Dollar threshold for campus audits.** We found that the dollar threshold for selecting some returns for campus audits has remained constant or has been adjusted informally based on inventory needs.[38] SB/SE has not evaluated whether the threshold should change or be changed more formally. According to officials, the dollar threshold is the break-even point for collecting enough tax to justify the audit. However, the threshold is only a guide; sometimes the threshold can be higher depending on how many returns need to be audited to meet the audit plan. According to one official, the threshold amount has been in place at least 4 years and possibly as long as 10 years.

- **Classification review.** We also found that classification decisions are not always required to be reviewed. For DIF and NRP returns, about 10 percent of classified returns are required to be reviewed for accuracy and adherence to classification guidelines. However, other field audit selection methods, including some referrals, do not include a formal classification quality review. Likewise, campus audit selections by analysts are not formally reviewed.

Internal Control Standard: Monitor controls

Program managers should have a strategy and procedures to continually monitor and assure the effectiveness of its control activities. Key duties and responsibilities should be divided among different people to reduce the risk of error and to achieve organizational goals. Program managers need operational data to determine whether they are meeting their strategic and annual performance plans and their goals for effective and efficient use of resources.

Source: GAO. | GAO-16-103

- **Review of group manager decisions.** SB/SE does not always require that group manager return selection decisions (i.e., screen- out) be reviewed. Even though multiple people are involved, in some cases, the group manager can independently make the final selection or screen-out decision. For state and agency referrals, and others to varying degrees, screen-out decisions by group managers are not reviewed. For example, in our file review of 30 screened-out returns, 8 were screened out by group managers. We did not see documentation of the approval for screening out these returns because such documentation was not required. According to SB/SE officials, group managers are the most knowledgeable about the resources available to meet audit goals. The managers also consult with territory and area managers to determine which returns should be screened out. For campus audits, approvals are not required to screen out returns from audit. Officials said that workload selection analysts communicate about the status of current and upcoming work to determine which returns are excess inventory and not needed to meet the annual audit plan or unable to be worked because of resource limitations.[39]

- **Source codes.** We found that some codes for identifying the return to be audited, called source codes, were mislabeled, not used, or not well defined, even though the IRM states that all data elements in IRS databases should be defined and documented.[40] In our review of 215 files, six returns were coded as non-Tax Equity and Fiscal Responsibility Act of 1982 (TEFRA) related pickups.[41] SB/SE officials later explained that these returns were mislabeled and should be moved to the source code used for TEFRA-related work. We also found two files that were coded as information referrals that should have been coded as related pickup audits, one file that was coded as a DIF-sourced return that should have been coded as a claim by a taxpayer to adjust a return he or she had filed, and three files that were coded as compliance initiative projects that should have been coded as returns selected to train auditors. For campus audits, source codes are assigned to each return audited but are not used to identify, select, or monitor campus inventory and do not serve any other purpose in campus audits. As a result, a source code may not represent the actual source of the inventory. Further, we found two source codes that were not well defined. One source code associated with about 35 percent of campus audits completed in fiscal year 2014 included references to DIF that were generally not applicable, since these returns were not related to or identified using DIF scoring. Another source code associated with about 13 percent of campus audits completed in fiscal year 2014 was labelled as two different items and did not accurately describe many of the returns using this code.[42]

Spreading responsibility for reviewing selection and screen-out decisions can reduce the potential for error and unfairness. In addition, adequate controls can help ensure that audits are appropriately coded so that IRS has accurate information to better ensure the efficient and effective use of resources. For example, having better controls on how returns are coded decreases the risk that data elements are misleading, which can hinder the decision-making process, such as prioritizing returns to select for audit and analyzing whether goals are met.

CONCLUSIONS

SB/SE relies on a variety of sources and processes to select returns for audit. This complexity underscores the importance of having a robust internal control system to support the selection process and achieve SB/SE's mission of administering the "tax law with integrity and fairness to all." SB/SE has some procedures in place that are consistent with internal control standards. However, we identified some internal control weaknesses that leave its audit program vulnerable to inconsistent return selection or the perception of it. Without effective internal controls, including defining fairness in selecting returns, SB/SE cannot know if it is achieving its mission and whether its return selection policies and procedures are aligned with its mission. Further, IRS will not be able to manage risk or monitor performance as well as it otherwise could. Finally, IRS risks the appearance that its return selection process is unfair to taxpayers because it is unable to communicate key pieces of information, such as its definition of fairness, to the public.

RECOMMENDATIONS FOR EXECUTIVE ACTION

To help ensure SB/SE's audit selection program meets its mission and selects returns fairly, we recommend that the Commissioner of Internal Revenue take the following actions:

- Clearly define and document the key term "fairness" for return selection activities.
- Clearly communicate examples of fair selections to staff to better assure consistent understanding.
- Develop, document, and implement program-level objective(s) to evaluate whether the return selection process is meeting its mission of applying the tax law with integrity and fairness to all.

To help ensure that SB/SE's audit selection objective(s) on fairness are used and met, we recommend that the Commissioner of Internal Revenue take the following actions:

- Develop, document, and implement related performance measures that would allow SB/SE to determine how well the selection of returns for audit meets the new objective(s).
- Incorporate the new objective(s) for fair return selection into the SB/SE risk management system to help identify and analyze potential risks to fair selections.

In addition, we recommend that the Commissioner of Internal Revenue take the following actions:

- Develop and implement consistent documentation requirements to clarify the reasons for selecting a return for audit and who reviewed and approved the selection decision.
- Develop, document, and implement monitoring procedures to ensure that decisions made and coding used to select returns for audit are appropriate.

AGENCY COMMENTS AND OUR EVALUATION

We provided a draft of this report to the Commissioner of Internal Revenue for review and comment. The Deputy Commissioner for Services and Enforcement provided written comments on November 23, 2015, which are reprinted in appendix VII. IRS stated that it agrees with the importance of sound internal controls and is committed to their improvement, especially in the areas we recommended. IRS stated that it agreed with our seven recommendations. Accordingly, the enclosure to the letter listed specific IRS actions planned to implement the recommendations. IRS also provided technical comments, which we incorporated where appropriate.

As IRS's letter mentioned, its audit program includes various features that are intended to promote fair return selection, such as documents that convey the importance of "fairness," existing objectives and measures, and types of monitoring. However, as our report discusses, these features do not clarify what fair selection of returns for audit entails and how IRS would know whether fair selections are occurring, except for when someone such as a taxpayer questions the fairness of return selection.

For our recommendations on defining and documenting "fairness" for return selection activities and communicating examples of fair selections to staff, IRS stated that the concept of fairness has both collective and individual attributes. IRS noted that fairness for return selection encompasses three components—pursuing those who fail to comply, objectively selecting noncompliant returns across all areas of noncompliance, and respecting and adhering to taxpayers' rights. As such, IRS has taken the first step to implement our recommendation. However, to fully implement our recommendation, IRS will need to clarify how each component relates to return selection. For example, the first and third components also cover what happens after return selection, such as pursuing noncompliance and interacting with taxpayers during the audit.

In regard to our recommendations on developing one or more program objectives and related measures on return selection related to fairness, as our report discusses, IRS's current program objectives and measures do not address fair selection of returns. We believe that IRS should develop at least one objective and related measure that tie to its definition of fairness. Doing so would allow IRS to more conclusively demonstrate and assess whether its selection decisions were fair.

We also recommended that IRS improve the documentation and monitoring of selection decisions. Our report acknowledges that documentation and monitoring does occur in many areas but provides examples of the need for more in other areas. As such, IRS needs additional documentation and monitoring as opposed to merely a plan to evaluate the need to take these actions.

We note three other clarifications based on statements in IRS's letter.

- First, IRS's letter correctly stated that our report did not identify any instances where the selection was considered inappropriate or unfair. We did not design our study to look for inappropriate and unfair selections, but rather to assess the internal controls that help ensure a fair selection process. Further, even if we did design our study to look for unfair selections, our design would be hampered by the lack of a definition for fairness and related objective(s) and measures(s) to evaluate whether selections were fair.
- Second, IRS's letter stated that the seven groupings in our report do not reflect how IRS views its workstreams for identifying returns for potential audit selection. As discussed in the report, our groupings are based on how a return was initially identified rather than on IRS's

workstreams. For example, related pickups, including DIF-related pickups, are identified by auditors, whereas DIF-selected returns are identified by a computer algorithm. Therefore, we separately grouped DIF-related pickups from DIF- selected returns. Furthermore, IRS could not provide complete data on the number of returns audited from each of its workstreams but could provide data on audits selected from other sources, such as related pickups. While some of these sources could be associated with a workstream, it was not possible for all. As a result, we used the available IRS data to show how all SB/SE audits were distributed by these audit identification workstreams and sources (shown in the report as figure 3).

- Third, DIF return selections do not involve the least amount of discretion, as IRS's letter stated. As discussed in our report, many returns that were initially identified through DIF automation as having audit potential were not audited. The actual audit selections do not occur until multiple IRS staff review those returns, requiring some human discretion. Our report discusses other groupings with less staff discretion than DIF, such as when taxpayers request that IRS review their returns or when IRS randomly selects returns for a research program.

James R. McTigue, Jr.
Director, Tax Issues
Strategic Issues

APPENDIX I: OBJECTIVES, SCOPE, AND METHODOLOGY

This report (1) describes the processes for selecting Small Business/Self-Employed (SB/SE) returns for audit, and (2) assesses how well the processes and controls for selecting those returns support SB/SE's mission of "applying the tax law with integrity and fairness to all."

For the first objective, we reviewed Internal Revenue Service (IRS) documents that describe the processes and criteria for selecting SB/SE returns for audit. These documents included sections of the Internal Revenue Manual (IRM), procedures documents, process flowcharts, and summaries of selection processes prepared by SB/SE officials. We also interviewed IRS officials responsible for overseeing audit selection. To provide information on closed IRS and SB/SE audits, we analyzed data for 2011 through 2014 from the

Compliance Data Warehouse Audit Information Management System (AIMS) closed table. We compared the results of our analyses of data in AIMS to the IRS data book to assess consistency of results. We determined that these data were sufficiently reliable for the purposes for which they were used in this engagement.

For the second objective, we reviewed SB/SE's procedures for selecting returns for audit and related internal controls intended to help SB/SE achieve its stated mission of "enforcing the tax law with integrity and fairness to all." We then assessed whether these procedures followed standards from *Standards for Internal Control in the Federal Government* that were relevant to return selection.[43] To determine which standards were most relevant, we used our *Internal Control Management and Evaluation Tool,* in conjunction with observations from our preliminary audit work.[44] We selected the most relevant internal control standards as criteria in consultation with SB/SE officials and our financial management and assurance and information technology teams.

We also conducted eight focus groups with selected SB/SE staff who are responsible for reviewing or selecting SB/SE returns for audit. We held two groups with field office staff who review returns for audit potential, two groups with area office staff who coordinate the review process, two groups with field office group managers who select returns for audit, one group with campus staff who review and select returns for audit, and one group with specialty tax group managers who select returns for audit. Within these five populations, we randomly selected participants who met our criteria of having more than 2 years of IRS work experience, working in different IRS offices nationwide, and covering a range of compliance issue areas. In total, our groups involved 58 participants with an average of about 9 years of IRS experience, with a range from 3 to 32 years of experience. The focus groups were held by telephone. We asked questions on internal control related topics, such as the clarity of SB/SE procedures and the adequacy of guidance to apply these procedures.

To assess the extent to which SB/SE implemented its procedures, we conducted a file review. We used IRM sections and SB/SE procedures documents as criteria. We obtained the population of SB/SE audits opened from March 2014 to February 2015 as shown in the open AIMS database and selected a nonprobability sample of 173 returns to review. Although the results of our file review cannot be projected to the population of SB/SE audits, they represent a variety of types of returns, sources, and selection processes. We focused on processes that required more manual review or affected a large number of taxpayers. As reflected in table 2, we reviewed more files for referrals and compliance initiative projects because they involve more human discretion in deciding whether to include the return in the selection inventory and in reviewing the returns for audit potential than for some other categories. We also reviewed more files for discriminant function (DIF) returns compared to some other categories because DIF returns are the largest portion of SB/SE's field audit workload by selection method or workstream. We reviewed the files to determine if decisions were documented and if staff followed procedures, such as documenting the rationale and approval for selecting or screening out returns. In sum, table 2 reflects the different types of returns we sampled, the type of files we reviewed, and the population and sample size of the files.

Table 2. Description of Samples to Review SB/SE Procedures for Selecting Returns to Audit

Sample category	Files reviewed	Unit of analysis	Population (audits opened March 2014 to February 2015)	Sample size
DIF and DIF-related pickups	Paper audit case files	Tax return	32,176	38
Non-DIF related pickups	Paper audit case files	Tax return	22,407	24
Compliance initiative projects (CIP)	Electronic CIP approval form and white paper	Tax return	1,638	30
Referrals	Paper audit case files and approval forms; electronic selection files	Tax return	20,474	56
Nonfiler	Paper audit case files; electronic selection files	Tax return	70,623	25
Classification review	Electronic Form 5126 Classification Quality Review Record	Classifier (auditor)	664	30
Survey (screened-out)	Paper case files	Tax return	27,563	30

Source: GAO analysis of IRS data. | GAO-16-103.

As shown in the last two rows of table 2, we also reviewed nongeneralizable, random samples of 30 returns that had been surveyed (i.e., screened out) and 30 classification quality review records for the same general time period as the audit files we reviewed. We created a separate sample of screened-out returns because audits were not opened on these returns. The database we used to create the audit file sample only contained returns that had been audited. We obtained the population of screened-out returns from SB/SE officials and randomly selected our sample from this population. We created a separate sample for classification quality review records because SB/SE reviews classification decisions per auditor rather than per return. We obtained the population of auditors that were reviewed during the same general time period as the files for the other samples. We identified subpopulations by region and selected a stratified random sample of these subpopulations.

Finally, we interviewed SB/SE officials about the procedures and discussed deficiencies we identified. We designed uniform data collection instruments for our file review to consistently capture information on the completeness of required documentation and approvals related to return selection. IRS reviewed the instruments and the data we captured. To ensure accuracy, two of our analysts reviewed each file we assessed and reconciled any differences in responses. We then analyzed the results of these data collection efforts to identify main themes and develop summary findings.

We conducted this performance audit from September 2014 to December 2015 in accordance with generally accepted government auditing standards. Those standards require that we plan and perform the audit to obtain sufficient, appropriate evidence to provide a reasonable basis for our findings and conclusions based on our audit objectives. We believe that the evidence obtained provides a reasonable basis for our findings and conclusions based on our audit objectives.

APPENDIX II: SUMMARY OF SMALL BUSINESS/SELF-EMPLOYED (SB/SE) AUDIT RESULTS, FISCAL YEAR 2014

Table 3. SB/SE Audits by Number, Amount of Recommended Additional Tax, Days to Conduct the Audit, and Direct Audit Hours Compared to All Internal Revenue Service (IRS) Audits, Fiscal Year 2014 (dollars in millions)

	Fiscal year 2014		
Characteristic	**All IRS audits**	**All SB/SE audits**	**Percent of SB/SE to IRS audits**
Number of audits closed	1,384,365	823,904	59.5%
Recommended additional tax	$33,149	$12,062	36.4%
Number of days to conduct an audit			
Mean	268	283	
Median	226	224	
Number of direct audit hours			
Mean	10	10	
Median	1	2	

Source: GAO analysis of IRS data. | GAO-16-103.

Note: Mean is the arithmetic average of the observed values of a continuous variable. Mean is calculated by adding all the values together and dividing the sum by the number of values. Median is the midpoint of a set of observed values arranged in either ascending or descending order.

Table 4. SB/SE Field and Campus Audits by Number, Amount of Recommended Additional Tax, Days to Conduct the Audit, and Direct Audit Hours Compared to All SB/SE Audits, Fiscal Year 2014 (dollars in millions)

		Fiscal year 2014			
		SB/SE closed field audits		SB/SE closed campus audits	
Characteristic	All SB/SE audits	Results	Percent of field to all SB/SE	Results	Percent of campus to all SB/SE
Number of audits closed	823,904	356,995	43.3%	466,909	56.7%
Recommended additional tax	$12,062	$7,597	63.0%	$4,465	37.0%
Number of days to conduct an audit					
Mean	283	310		262	
Median	224	256		212	
Number of direct audit hours					
Mean	10	22		1	
Median	2	10		1	

Source: GAO analysis of IRS data. | GAO-16-103.

Note: Mean is the arithmetic average of the observed values of a continuous variable. Mean is calculated by adding all the values together and dividing the sum by the number of values. Median is the midpoint of a set of observed values arranged in either ascending or descending order.

Appendix III: Description of Small Business/Self-Employed (SB/SE) Selection Methods or Workstreams

1. **Area Office Referral -** Area office field personnel refer potential leads with correspondence audit issues to Campus Reporting Compliance (CRC).
2. **Audit Information Management Systems (AIMS)/AIMS Computer Information System (A-CIS)/Previously Adjusted Exam Issues on Subsequent-year Filings -** Quarterly A-CIS reports are run to identify every campus case closed agreed or default in each of the discretionary audit programs. The subsequent year returns are classified for the same issues that are on the closed audit cases.
3. **Audit Reconsideration -** Reevaluates the results of a prior audit where additional tax was assessed and remains unpaid, or a tax credit was reversed. IRS also uses the process when the taxpayer contests a Substitute for Return determination by filing an original delinquent return.
4. **Campus Reporting Compliance (CRC) Compliance Initiative Project (CIP) Usage -** CRC uses CIP Authorization (Form 13498) to document approval for testing potential new inventory in correspondence audits.
5. **Category A Claims for Refund -** Accounts Management staff refer claims for refunds that meet criteria indicating audit potential directly to Classification and Claim Teams within the campuses.
6. **Criminal Investigation Referral -** CRC uses IRS's databases to determine if the issues Criminal Investigation identified exist on the referred returns.
7. **Claim -** A request for refund or an adjustment of tax paid or credit not previously reported or allowed.
8. **Collection Referral -** CRC receives two kinds of referrals from collection each year. CRC receives three referrals yearly of potential nonfiler leads from the collection queue. CRC also receives occasional referrals of Form 3949 Information Item referrals.
9. **Compliance Data Environment Release 3** - Identifies potential audits through user-defined filters and queries, and forwards those selected to the correct treatment stream.

10. **Compliance Data Warehouse/Potential Unreported Heavy Use Tax -** Identifies Form 2290 returns (Heavy Highway Vehicle Use Tax Return) with potential unreported heavy use tax.
11. **Compliance Initiative Project (CIP) –** When IRS identifies potential noncompliance in specific groups of taxpayers, CIPs are used to contact or audit taxpayers or collect taxpayer data within that group when another method to identify such workload is not already in place.
12. **Discriminant Function (DIF) -** A mathematical technique to estimate or "score" the potential merit of auditing a particular tax return based on its characteristics.
13. **Discretionary Exam Business Rules (DEBR) -** DEBR rules were developed to identify non-Earned Income Tax Credit returns with the highest audit potential for additional tax assessment for certain return conditions.
14. **Employee Audit -** Any employee selected for audit under any and all methods of inventory identification (e.g., DIF (see definition above), referrals). It also includes inventory that is specifically identified based on the individual's position within IRS. Inventory identification is designed to ascertain compliance among IRS employees while maintaining their right to privacy.
15. **Employment Tax Referral -** Specialty tax personnel refer potential audit leads relating to possible unfiled payroll tax returns to CRC (see definition above).
16. **Estate & Gift Tax Form 1041** - Filters identify Form 1041 returns reporting charitable contributions, fiduciary fees, and other miscellaneous deductions.
17. **Estate & Gift (E&G) Referrals -** E&G tax personnel refer potential audit leads relating to possible unreported executor fees to CRC.
18. **Government Liaison and Disclosure (GLD) Referrals -** GLD personnel refer information to CRC from sources outside IRS, such as states and the Puerto Rican Tax Authority (see definition below), that are potential audit leads.
19. **High Income Nonfiler -** Strategy designed to address the filing compliance of taxpayers with known sources of income exceeding $200,000.
20. **Information Reports -** Reports and referrals that may include information on substantial civil tax potential and significant potential

for fraud, or are related to returns for tax years not yet required to be filed.

21. **National Research Program (NRP) -** A comprehensive effort by IRS to measure compliance for different types of taxes and various sets of taxpayers. It provides a statistically valid representation of the compliance characteristics of taxpayers.
22. **Offers-In-Compromise/Doubt as to Liability -** An offer in compromise is an agreement between the taxpayer and IRS that settles a tax debt for less than the full amount owed. Doubt as to liability exists where there is a genuine dispute as to the existence or amount of the correct tax debt under the law.
23. **Payment Card Income Pilot -** Potential underreporters are flagged when Form 1099-K receipts, as a portion of gross receipts, are significantly greater than for similar taxpayers, suggesting cash underreporting.
24. **Promoter Investigations and Client Returns -** SB/SE auditors, as well as other IRS or external sources, refer potentially abusive transaction promoters/preparers for audit. Client returns are audited to determine whether penalties and/or an injunction are warranted.
25. **Puerto Rican Tax Authority Nonfiler -** The Puerto Rican Tax Authority provides information to IRS through the Government Liaison Office about residents in Puerto Rico who fail to file their federal tax return.
26. **Research Referral -** Research personnel refer potential audit leads relating to NRP, possible nonfilers, and problem preparers to CRC.
27. **Return Preparer Program Action Cases and Client Returns -** Clients of questionable preparers are audited to determine whether preparer penalties and/or injunctive actions are warranted. These are limited to preparer misconduct or incompetence that is pervasive and widespread.
28. **Submissions Processing -** Submission Processing staff refer potential audit leads relating to the Alternative Minimum Tax program, math error, and unallowables to CRC or campus classifiers.
29. **State Audit Referral Program (SARP) -** SARP utilizes the audit report information submitted to IRS by various taxing agencies to address areas of noncompliance.
30. **State/Other Agency Referral -** Federal, state, and local governmental agencies share relationships and data with IRS through

the Governmental Liaison staff to increase compliance levels, reduce the tax gap, reduce taxpayer burden, and optimize use of resources.

31. **Treasury Inspector General for Tax Administration (TIGTA) Referral** - TIGTA personnel refer potential audit leads relating to TIGTA investigations to CRC.
32. **Tip Program Referral** - Employees who do not report at or above the tip rate as agreed upon by the employer under various agreements with IRS may be referred for audit.
33. **Whistleblower Claim** - Allegations of violation of federal tax laws made by a person who requests a reward.

Source: GAO analysis of IRS information. | GAO-16-103

APPENDIX IV: SMALL BUSINESS/SELF EMPLOYED (SB/SE) SELECTION METHODS BY BROAD IDENTIFICATION SOURCE

Table 5 shows the selection methods or workstreams by how the returns were identified.

Table 5. SB/SE Selection Methods or Workstreams by Broad Identification Source

Identification source	Description of identification	Field methods or workstreams	Campus methods or workstreams
Referrals to Internal Revenue Service (IRS) audit offices	IRS employees and units, as well as external sources, such as other agencies and citizens, can refer potentially noncompliant taxpayers to SB/SE. SB/SE may start an audit if the referral indicates significant potential for noncompliance.	**Internal and external to IRS** Employee audits Information reports Promoter investigations and client returns Return preparer program action cases and client returns **External to IRS** State/other agency	**Internal to IRS** Area office (nonfiler) Collection (nonfiler) Criminal Investigation Employment tax Estate tax (executor fee) Government Liaison and Disclosure

Identification source	Description of identification	Field methods or workstreams	Campus methods or workstreams
		Whistleblower claim	(Puerto Rico claims and international) Research Submissions processing (Alternative Minimum Tax) Tip Program[a] **External to IRS** Treasury Inspector General for Tax Administration State audit referral program[a] Puerto Rican tax agency nonfiler
Related pickups	After opening an audit, SB/SE may identify the taxpayer's prior or subsequent year returns or returns of related taxpayers to audit.	Various workstreams	Various workstreams
User-defined criteria	These criteria use filters or rules embedded in computer software to identify returns with specific characteristics, often for projects. These characteristics generally involve a specific tax issue known or suspected to have high noncompliance in a particular geographic area, industry, or population.	Compliance initiative project High income nonfiler Compliance Data Environment Release 3	Compliance initiative project Potential unreported heavy use tax Estate and gift tax form 1041 (certain expenses)

Table 5. (Continued)

Identification source	Description of identification	Field methods or workstreams	Campus methods or workstreams
Computer program	Computer programs use rules or formulas to identify potential noncompliance across a type of tax return, rather than for a specific tax issue.	Discriminant function	Audit Information Management Systems Computer Information System-Previously adjusted exam issues on subsequent year fillings Discretionary exam business rules[a]
Data matching	When information on a tax return—such as wages, interest, and dividends—does not match information reported to IRS by states, employers, or other third parties, these discrepancies may prompt SB/SE to review returns for audit potential.	Payment card income pilot	Payment card income pilot
Taxpayer initiated	When taxpayers contact IRS to request an adjustment to their respective tax returns, tax refunds, or tax credits, or ask to have a previous audit reconsidered, SB/SE may initiate an audit after reviewing these requests.	Audit reconsideration Claims Offer-in-Compromise/Doubt as to Liability	Category A Claims
Random identification	The National Research Program (NRP) studies tax compliance through	NRP	NRP

Identification source	Description of identification	Field methods or workstreams	Campus methods or workstreams
	audits of a randomly-identified sample of tax returns. Specifically, NRP measures voluntary compliance in reporting income, deductions, credits, among other categories, and generalizes those measures to the population being studied.		

Source: GAO analysis of IRS information. | GAO-16-103.

Notes: Certain workload can come from different sources. For example, employee audits can be initiated through internal and external referrals, as well as other sources. We categorized based on how IRS characterized the workload identification method or the most frequent source. Referrals can originate from automated sources, as well as individuals. SB/SE's specialty tax (employment, excise, and estate and gift tax) returns are also identified for audit from these seven identification sources. In addition to audits, SB/SE conducts compliance reviews, which we have not included in this table or scope of this review. We also omitted frivolous return program because it moved from SB/SE to the Wage and Investment (W&I) division as of November 2014.

[a] SB/SE manages this workload after realignment from W&I in November 2014.

APPENDIX V: EXAMPLES OF SIMILARITIES AND VARIATIONS ACROSS SELECTION METHODS

Figures 4 and 5 represent general similarities and variations in the Small Business/Self-Employed (SB/SE) return selection process at its field and campus locations, respectively. They do not include every process that occurs in the various methods or workstreams. In addition, the phases and processes in the figures are not necessarily discrete events but may overlap and involve other processes and staff.

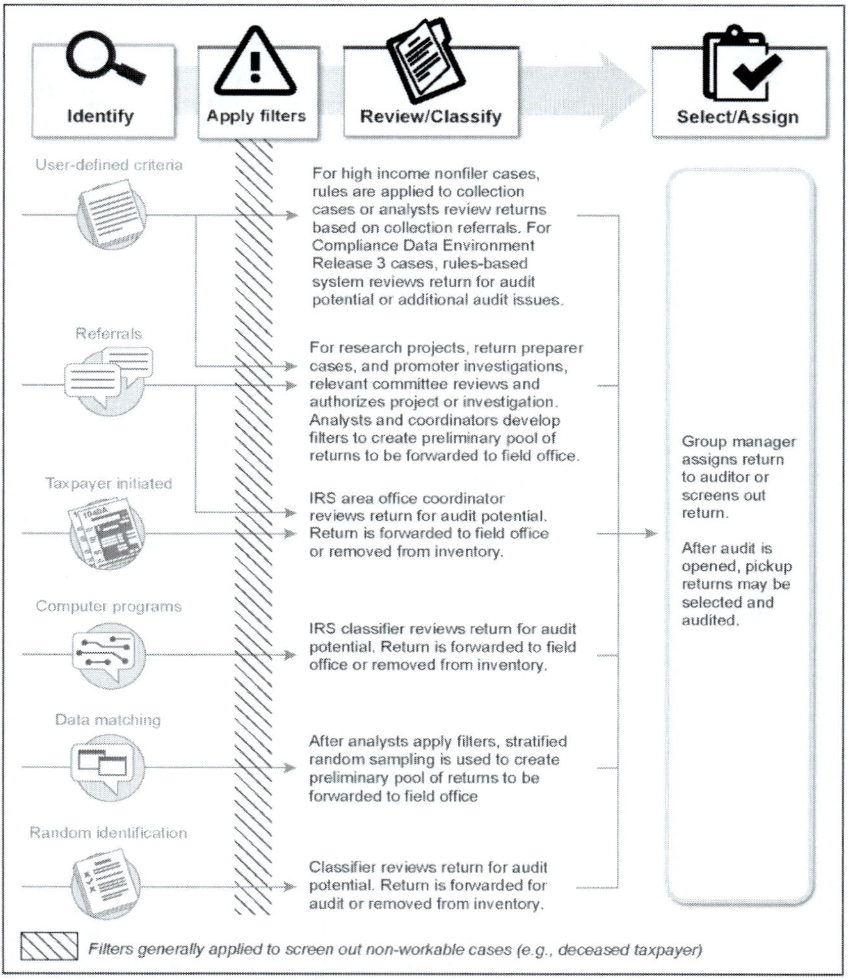

Source: GAO analysis of IRS information. | GAO-16-103

Figure 4. Example of Selection Processes for Internal Revenue Service (IRS) SB/SE Field Audits.

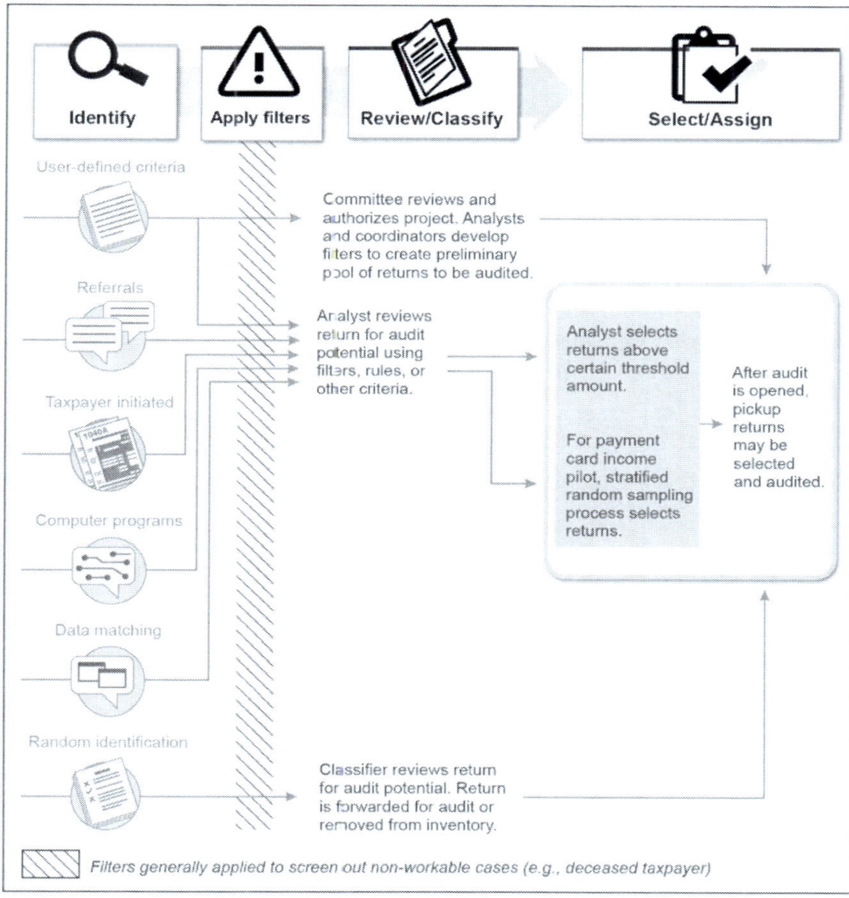

Source: GAO analysis of IRS information. | GAO-16-103.

Figure 5. Example of Selection Processes for IRS SB/SE Campus Audits.

Appendix VI: Small Business/Self-Employed (SB/SE) Field Audit Sources and Audit Information Management System (AIMS) Source Codes

The AIMS source code indicates the initial source of how the return was identified for audit. Table 6 shows the number of field audits closed by source code and by grouping of source codes into categories for fiscal year 2014.

Table 6. SB/SE Field Audits by Number and Internal Revenue Service (IRS) AIMS Source Code, Fiscal Year 2014

		Category for field audits			
Source code	**Description**	**Number of closed SB/SE field audits**	**Source code category**	**Number of closed audits by category**	**Percent of category to all closed field audits**
02	Discriminant Function(DIF) returns	69,711			
20, project code 0158	Regular (manual) classification -DIF return	10,382			
Subtotal			**DIF**	**80,093**	**22.4%**
05	DIF –filed return related to primary DIF return	16,327			
10	DIF –filed prior and/or subsequent return related to a primary DIF return	44,724			
12	DIF –nonfiled delinquent return or Substitute for Return (SFR) related to a primary DIF return	7,134			
39	Non-DIF –Tax shelter related pickup	2,852			
40	Non-DIF –Tax shelter related, filed prior and/or subsequent return pickup	51,950			
44	Non-DIF –Tax shelter related, nonfiled delinquent return or SFR	36,309			

		Category for field audits			
Source code	Description	Number of closed SB/SE field audits	Source code category	Number of closed audits by category	Percent of category to all closed field audits
50	Non-DIF –Filed return with different taxpayer identification number or master file transaction	17,241			
64	Non-DIF –Non-Tax Equity and Fiscal Responsibility Act (TEFRA) pickup related to Forms 1065, 1041, and 1120S other than tax shelter	96			
72	Related to a specialist referral	2,706			
88	Fraud -Special enforcement	240			
Subtotal			**Pickups**	**179,579**	**50.3%**
17	Tax shelter program	13,105			
49	Miscellaneous Non-DIF –return preparers	6,601			
60	Information reports	2,642			
65	Collection	54			
70	Other agency requests	1,340			
71	Specialist	422			
77	State information	278			
Subtotal			**Referrals**	**24,442**	**6.8%**
80	Research and Reference –National Research Program (NRP) - current		12,564		
91	Research and Reference -NRP-related returns		10,967		
Subtotal			**NRP**	**23,531**	**6.6%**
30	Claims -Claim for refund/abatement		10,018		
31	Claims -Paid claims for refund		444		
32	Claims -Carryback refund		619		
73	Miscellaneous non-DIF -Taxpayer requests		8,211		

Table 6. (Continued)

		Category for field audits			
Source code	**Description**	**Number of closed SB/SE field audits**	**Source code category**	**Number of closed audits by category**	**Percent of category to all closed field audits**
Subtotal			**Claims**	**19,292**	**5.4%**
01	Tax shelter returns - computer identified		580		
03	Unallowable items		60		
06	Correspondence audit –DIF		396		
08	Self-employment tax		14		
11	Research and Reference -Studies, Tests and Research		1,415		
20 (non-project code 0158)	Regular (manual) classification -other than DIF		9,165		
23	TEFRA related		25		
24	Nonfiler –local sourced work		4,675		
25	Nonfiler –Strategic initiative		1,355		
26	Minimum tax program		13		
35	Other -administrative adjustment request		12		
46	Miscellaneous non-DIF -Employee returns		185		
62	Miscellaneous non-DIF –Compliance Initiative Project		9,938		
85	Information Return Program information document match		11		
89	Fraud -Special enforcement-related		746		
90	Fraud –regular		1,457		
04	Multiple filers				
14	High underreporter		11[a]		
Subtotal			**All other**	**30,058**	**8.4%**
	Total – all field audits			**356,995**	**100.0%**

Source: GAO analysis of IRS data. | GAO-16-103.

[a] Values for individual source codes are suppressed to avoid identification of taxpayers

APPENDIX VII: COMMENTS FROM THE INTERNAL REVENUE SERVICE

DEPARTMENT OF THE TREASURY
INTERNAL REVENUE SERVICE
WASHINGTON, D.C. 20224

DEPUTY COMMISSIONER

November 23, 2015

James R. McTigue, Jr.
Director, Tax Policy and Administration
Strategic Issues Team
U.S. Government Accountability Office
441 G Street NW Washington, DC 20548

Dear Mr. McTigue:

Thank you for the opportunity to comment on the draft report titled, *IRS RETURN SELECTION: Certain Internal Controls for Audits in the Small Business and Self-Employed Division Should Be Strengthened (GAO-16-103)*. We appreciate that GAO recognized that IRS has procedures that adhere to internal control standards and provide a level of assurance of fairness and integrity in the return selection process. The report notes that the Small Business/Self Employed Division (SB/SE) demonstrated a commitment to promoting ethical behavior among staff and that there is an awareness of internal control procedures by managers which is important to achieving our mission. The report also found that segregation of duties in the return selection process means that no individual can control the decision-making process and that there are safeguards in place to restrict access to our systems to only authorized users.

The mission of the SB/SE Division is to help small business and self-employed taxpayers understand and meet their tax obligations while applying tax law with integrity and fairness to all. The terms integrity and fairness originate from the IRS Mission statement and all IRS employees, not just those involved in return selection, are expected to carry out their duties with integrity and fairness to all.

Your report states that IRS has not defined fairness or program objectives for audit selection and corresponding performance measures, which leaves its audit program vulnerable to inconsistent return selection or the perception of it. In the SB/SE Examination sphere, the concept of fairness has both a collective and individual component. The IRS takes into account the responsibilities and obligations that all taxpayers share. We pursue those individuals and businesses who fail to comply with their tax obligations to ensure fairness to those who do and to promote public confidence in our tax system, and we discharge these important responsibilities with a focus on taxpayer rights, as embodied in the Taxpayer Bill of Rights (TBOR) and formally adopted by IRS.

Indeed, as reflected in our Policy Statement 4-21, the objective in selecting returns for examination is to promote the highest degree of voluntary compliance on the part of taxpayers through equitably selecting returns which indicate the probability of substantial error. As your report indicates, SB/SE has procedures in place that meet several internal control standards and provide assurance of fairness and integrity in the return selection process. These critical assurances are ensured by design of the overall process – they are embedded into the foundation of our selection processes, which is designed to objectively select returns with the highest probability of noncompliance by relying on a combination of automated processes, historical data, scoring mechanisms, and data-driven algorithms; and the entire process operates under a comprehensive set of checks and balances and safeguards, all aimed at delivering a process that is fair and equitable by design.

In addition, SB/SE has multiple program level objectives with corresponding performance measures that ensure taxpayers are treated fairly. All employees are evaluated on how well they provide fair and equitable treatment to taxpayers as required by the Internal Revenue Service Restructuring and Reform Act of 1998. This includes employees involved with return selection. Moreover, fairness is embodied in the IRS's approach to taxpayer rights, a responsibility that we take seriously and that is a priority for all IRS employees in their work every day. Many of the rights in the TBOR, a cornerstone document that provides the nation's taxpayers with a better understanding of their rights, are aimed at ensuring that we discharge our mission with fairness and integrity (including, for example, the right to be informed, the right to finality, privacy and confidentiality).

We note that, while your report posits a hypothetical risk to fair case selection from the lack of documented objectives and internal control deficiencies, your report did not identify any instances where the selection of a case was considered inappropriate or unfair. Your report cites employee focus group comments as demonstrating that employees have an inconsistent understanding of fairness in return selection. Ignoring geographic location in return selection is not incompatible with considering geography to avoid examinations of taxpayers that one may know. Both are indications that we consider fairness in selection. The first attempts to balance coverage across the country, and the second attempts to avoid any appearance of bias. Also, we note that fairness of the return selection process is not an individual employee responsibility – it is the responsibility of upper management to design a process that ensures a fair and objective selection of noncompliant cases. The employees' role with respect to fairness is to perform their duties in a manner that respects and protects taxpayers' rights. We will continue, as we already do, to monitor any claims or situations where there is a question of fairness in return selection; and we will refer to the Treasury Inspector General for Tax Administration any taxpayer complaints that relate to fairness in return selection.

SB/SE has conducted both formal and informal risk assessments of its audit selection procedures as part of longstanding, routine internal controls procedures. For example, all levels of management conduct business performance reviews, annual assurance reviews, and operational reviews. Reviews at the group, territory, area, and headquarters levels are all used as opportunities to formally identify risks, not only in the case selection process but in all aspects of our operations. In addition, the Chief Risk Officer completed a risk based review of the IRS Audit Selection Process in March 2014 with participation from exam functions within SB/SE. To facilitate the review, a standardized template for each examination workstream was prepared that provided the specific steps and individual roles utilized to approve, operationalize and maintain the workstream. The results of this review substantiated that we consistently maintain sound internal controls throughout our examination programs.

Your report cites the lack of documentation for some return selection decisions as an area of internal control weakness. It specifically mentions the decision to "screen out" a previously selected return as an example of this lack of documentation. Since this activity occurs after the return has been identified and selected, we do not consider this as part of the return selection process. Cases are not screened out because they do not have a possible compliance issue; they are screened out due to other factors such as resource constraints or priority of the workload.

Your report also outlines improvements for the monitoring of the decisions that are made and the coding for return selections. SB/SE Field Examination regularly monitors the application of coding and periodically performs a 100% inventory validation. This includes the requirement that all returns be physically reviewed to ensure they are accurately coded and, if errors are found, corrections are made. However, we agree improvements can be made, specifically in the area of coding SB/SE Campus Examination returns and appropriate actions will be taken.

As described in the draft report, the SB/SE Examination return selection process relies on a variety of sources and processes to select returns for audit. SB/SE has 33 different workstreams (or types of work); all of which follow a general, multiphase process for identifying, classifying and selecting returns for examination. Within this process, there are some variations across the workstreams. For example, there are more automated processes for campus selections and more manual processes for some field selections where the case work is more complex.

We believe the seven groupings used in your report to describe our workstreams do not provide an accurate picture of our sources of work. For example, related pickups is not a category of work from a workstream perspective and the use of this grouping is misleading. The least amount of discretion is exercised in Discriminant Index Function (DIF) return selections. Including DIF pickups in this grouping, implies that a majority of our work is selected based upon non-automated factors, which is simply not accurate. A

DIF sourced initial return is the source of the related pickup because without the primary DIF indicator, the related, prior or subsequent year returns would only have been introduced into the audit workstream if they were independently identified by DIF.

We agree with the importance of sound internal controls and are committed to their improvement; especially in the areas that your report recommends that we strengthen them. We agree with your recommendations, and the enclosure provides additional detail on the specific IRS actions planned to implement them. In closing, we appreciate and value your continued support and insight as we strive to further strengthen our processes and programs throughout the Service. If you have any questions, please contact me, or a member of your staff may contact Karen Schiller, Commissioner, Small Business/Self Employed Division, at (202) 317-0600.

Sincerely,

John M. Dalrymple
Deputy Commissioner for Services and Enforcement

Enclosure

Enclosure

IRS RETURN SELECTION: Controls for Audits in the Small Business and Self-Employed Division Should Be Strengthened (GAO-16-103)

Recommendations for Executive Action

To help ensure SB/SE's audit selection program meets its mission and selects returns fairly, we recommend that the Commissioner of Internal Revenue take the following actions:

Recommendation 1: Clearly define and document the key term "fairness" for return selection activities.

Comment: Fairness for return selection activities has three components – fairness to the taxpaying public by pursuing those who fail to comply or otherwise meet their tax obligations, a fair process that objectively selects noncompliant returns for examination across all areas of noncompliance, and fairness to the individual taxpayers who are being examined by respecting and adhering to taxpayers' rights. These definitions of fairness are separately documented in our Policy Statement 4-21 and reflected in the IRS Taxpayer Bill of Rights (TBOR). We agree with your recommendation as to the value of documenting these definitions in a single document and we will take appropriate action to do so.

Recommendation 2: Clearly communicate examples of fair selections to staff to better assure consistent understanding.

Comment: SB/SE Examination will communicate to managers and examiners involved in the return selection examples of fairness in the return selection process and incorporate these examples into our training materials, as needed, to further ensure a consistent understanding of fairness.

Recommendation 3: Develop, document, and implement program-level objective(s) to evaluate whether the return selection process is meeting its mission of applying the tax law with integrity and fairness to all.

Comment: SB/SE will review current objectives for the Examination program priorities and identify and implement any additional objectives, as needed, addressing the return selection process.

Recommendation 4: Develop, document, and implement related performance measures that would allow SB/SE to determine how well the selection of returns for audit meets the new objective(s).

Comment: Many of our existing performance measures provide key indicators and insight as to our program performance with respect to fairness, including for example, the rate of examinations resulting in changes proposed to the reported tax, cycle time for the examination, and yield from the examination. During SB/SE's review of current objectives for recommendation #3, if new objectives are identified and implemented, SB/SE will develop, document, and implement any additional performance measures that are needed to assess achievement of the new objective(s).

Recommendation 5: Incorporate the new objective(s) for fair return selection into the SB/SE risk management system to help identify and analyze potential risks to fair selections.

Comment: The current SB/SE risk process requires identifying and assessing risks to business objectives. Any new objectives that are developed in response to recommendation #3 will be considered within the current SB/SE risk management process framework.

Recommendation 6: Develop and implement consistent documentation requirements to clarify the reasons for selecting a return for audit and who reviewed and approved the selection decision.

Comment: SB/SE Examination will evaluate the need to improve the documentation of decisions for return selection and for the review and approval process of the selection decisions made.

Recommendation 7: Develop, document, and implement monitoring procedures to ensure that decisions made and coding used to select returns for audit are appropriate.

Comment: SB/SE Examination will review current procedures for monitoring decisions made and coding used to select returns for audit and identify and implement any new procedures, if needed, to ensure coding of returns selected for audit is appropriate.

End Notes

[1] This population of taxpayers includes 41 million self-employed individuals, 9 million small corporations, and 7 million other taxpayers.

[2] An IRS audit (also called "examination") is a review of a taxpayer's books and records to determine whether information such as income, expenses, and credits are being reported accurately. Internal Revenue Code section 7602 gives the Secretary of the Department of the Treasury, IRS's parent agency, the authority to conduct audits.

[3] In January 2012, IRS estimated that the gross tax gap was $450 billion in tax year 2006 (the most current estimate available). IRS estimated that it would eventually recover about $65 billion of the gross tax gap through late payments and enforcement actions, leaving an annual estimated net tax gap of about $385 billion.

[4] GAO, *Small Businesses: IRS Considers Taxpayer Burden in Tax Administration, but Needs a Plan to Evaluate the Use of Payment Card Information for Compliance Efforts,* GAO-15-513 (Washington, D.C.: June 30, 2015).

[5] Internal Revenue Manual (IRM) Part 1, Chapter 1, Section 16.1 (http://www.irs.gov/irm/) states SB/SE's mission.

[6] This report is part of a larger body of our work on audit and collection case selection across IRS. See GAO, *IRS Case Selection: Automated Collection System Lacks Key Internal Controls Needed to Ensure the Program Fulfills Its Mission,* GAO-15-744 (Washington, D.C.: September 13, 2015); *IRS Case Selection: Collection Process Is Largely Automated, but Lacks Adequate Internal Controls,* GAO-15-647 (Washington, D.C.: July 29, 2015); and *IRS Examination Selection: Internal Controls for Exempt Organization Selection Should Be Strengthened,* GAO-15-514 (Washington, D.C.: July 13, 2015). Concerns about fairness were raised in the report, Treasury Inspector General for Tax Administration, *Inappropriate Criteria Were Used to Identify Tax-Exempt Applications for Review*, 2013-10-053 (Washington, D.C: May 14, 2013).

[7] See GAO, *Standards for Internal Control in the Federal Government*, GAO/AIMD-00-21.3.1 (Washington, D.C.: November 1999). A newer version of the standards (see GAO, *Standards for Internal Control in the Federal Government*, GAO-14-704G (Washington, D.C.: September 2014)) took effect in fiscal year 2016. Because we conducted our review mainly in fiscal year 2015, we used the new standards only as context in preparing for an effective internal control system in the future, not as criteria to evaluate the current controls.

[8] IRS uses the term "survey" to refer to the process of screening out returns after additional reviews reveal a reason not to conduct the audit. See IRM Part 4, Chapter 1, Section 3.6.

[9] Campuses, formerly called service centers, are facilities where IRS performs various operations, such as processing tax returns, handling taxpayer calls, and conducting correspondence audits.

[10] These data for all IRS audits exclude excise tax returns filed with the U.S. Customs and Border Protection and the Alcohol and Tobacco Tax and Trade Bureau; returns of tax- exempt organizations, government entities, employee retirement benefit plans, and tax- exempt bonds; and information returns.

[11] IRS: *Risk-Based Review of IRS Audit Selection Processes and Criteria*, Mar. 4, 2014.

[12] For campus audits, returns generally are not further reviewed by managers before starting the audit. After returns are selected for audit, taxpayers are notified, and auditors are assigned the return after taxpayers respond.

[13] According to IRS officials, a workstream is a category or major type of work. Appendix III describes the workstreams.

[14] Auditors identify related pickups when auditing another return, called the primary return. The primary return is identified through various methods or workstreams, including automated sources.

[15] Referrals of nonfilers can come from IRS staff, such as those involved with collecting unpaid tax debts, and from automated IRS systems.

[16] For information on IRS's plan for evaluating the payment card income pilot, see GAO-15-513.

[17] IRS's NRP is an effort to measure taxpayer compliance for strategic planning and budget purposes. IRS uses NRP data to estimate the tax gap and update formulas used to identify tax returns for potential audits.

[18] Some workstreams, such as NRP, allow few returns to be screened out. Returns identified for NRP cannot be screened out unless the taxpayer meets exclusionary criteria (e.g., death or natural disaster).

[19] We did not attempt to describe every variation across workstreams. Appendix V includes high-level flowcharts of the selection process and provides examples of some of these similarities and differences.

[20] We have shown certain workstreams or identification groups to better illustrate SB/SE's workload for field audits. IRS could not provide the number of closed audits by identification groups we developed. Therefore, to estimate the number of SB/SE closed audits by selection workstream or identification group, we used IRS Audit Information Management System source codes. We grouped these codes into the workstreams or identification groups shown in figure 3 and further described them in appendix VI.

[21] Congress established EITC in 1975. It is used to (1) offset the impact of Social Security taxes on low-income families and (2) encourage low-income families to seek employment rather than public assistance. Generally, credit amounts depend on the number of qualifying children who meet age, relationship, and residency tests. 26 U.S.C. § 32. As we have reported, root causes of EITC noncompliance are that taxpayers or their tax return preparers determine eligibility and that IRS has limited ability to verify eligibility before issuing refunds. See GAO, *Fiscal Outlook: Addressing Improper Payments and the Tax Gap Would Improve the Government's Fiscal Position*, GAO-16-92T (Washington, D.C.: Oct.1, 2015). IRS focuses on EITC because of noncompliance in claiming EITC. For fiscal year 2014, IRS estimates a 27 percent noncompliance rate and $17.7 billion in noncompliance.

[22] IRS reviews more returns than are selected for audit to ensure that it has enough returns that are ready to be audited when auditors are available. To determine how many returns need to be reviewed, IRS uses criteria to determine which returns have the most audit potential. We did not assess how IRS developed these criteria, whether IRS adhered to them, or their effectiveness because the processes were out of the scope of this review.

[23] See GAO/AIMD-00-21.3.1.

[24] We excluded areas where our other audit teams have reviewed internal controls. For example, a recent report highlighted weaknesses with controls in IRS's information security program. See GAO, *Information Security: IRS Needs to Continue Improving Controls over Financial and Taxpayer Data*, GAO-15-337 (Washington, D.C.: Mar. 19, 2015).

[25] This discussion excludes our results from assessing certain procedures—delegating responsibilities, applying outside evaluations, and responding to recommendations—that appeared to adhere to internal control standards. However, the documentation on their adherence to the standards was not as clear as for the four procedures cited above in the report.

[26] See IRM Part 4, Chapter 1, Section 5.1.20(1), and Chapter 10, Section 1.4(1), Section 1.6.10(1), and Section 1.6.10(2)(i).

[27] Classification is the process of reviewing a return to determine if it may merit an audit.

[28] The briefing references IRS's purpose to collect the proper amount of tax at the least cost to the public so as to foster confidence in IRS's integrity and fairness (IRM, Part 4, Chapter 1, Section 5.1.20(1)). The briefing also reviews IRM 4.1.5 on classification, national and local classification instructions, and expectations for the classification detail.

[29] According to officials, SB/SE is striving to achieve a balance between ensuring a minimum rate of audit coverage across all the return types and doing more audits of some return types to address the areas of highest taxpayer noncompliance. This approach may address concerns about fairness across taxpayer groups, which SB/SE could incorporate into its definition of fairness. However, officials also said that this balance can shift based on changes in various factors, such as emerging issues and resource availability. These changes in the factors illustrate the need to clarify what fair return selection means to maintain this "balance."

[30] A random sample of closed field audits is selected for this survey. Surveys ask taxpayers/representatives questions, most of which focus on with how satisfied they are with actions during the audit. For January 2015 to March 2015, IRS had an overall response rate of 18 percent. For the explanation the auditor provided on the reason for (a) the audit—55 percent of respondents were satisfied—and (b) an expanded audit scope—49 percent of respondents were satisfied.

[31] Pub. L. No. 105-206, §1204(b), 112 Stat. 685, 722 (1998). Examples of behaviors include timeliness in responding to taxpayers; discussing specific taxpayers with other staff only on a "need-to-know" basis; responding to taxpayers with appropriate tone, courtesy and respect; and stating facts accurately. See IRM Part 1, Chapter 5, Section 3.7.3.

[32] As part of the ERM process, SB/SE has established a risk committee and developed a preliminary risk register. We found four risks in SB/SE's risk register that directly or indirectly involved return selection.

[33] Risk tolerance is the acceptable level of variation in performance related to achieving objectives.

[34] For mandatory work, such as nationally-coordinated research projects and some employee audits, group managers are required to explain the screen-out decision.

[35] File review results are based on a nongeneralizable sample of SB/SE audits and are not representative of the population of SB/SE audits. Although nongeneralizable, the sample was taken to ensure coverage over a wide variety of audit types. For more information on our file review methodology, see appendix I.

[36] We requested documentation for our file review from April 2015 to June 2015 and reviewed the majority of the files from June 2015 to August 2015. We accepted files for review up to early October 2015.

[37] IRM Part 1, Chapter 15, Section 1.4.

[38] We are not reporting a specific dollar threshold because doing so could impair IRS's efforts to enforce the tax laws.

[39] Workload selection analysts order, review, select, and route the inventory of returns for campus audits.

[40] IRM Part 2, Chapter 5, Section 13.1.

[41] Pub. L. No. 97-248, §§ 401–407, 96 Stat. 324, 648–671 (1982). TEFRA established unified audit procedures for covered partnerships. A partnership was covered under these procedures if at any time during the year it had (1) more than 10 partners or (2) certain types of partners such as another partnership, a limited liability company that files as a partnership, and any type of trust, a nominee, a nonresident alien individual, among others. In November 2015, these provisions were repealed and replaced with new partnership audit procedures applicable to tax years starting after December 31, 2017. Pub. L. No. 114-74, § 1101 129 Stat. (2015).

[42] IRS describes source code 06 as DIF Correspondence, which are returns converted from other programs related to high DIF-scored returns or to request returns related to a DIF return

being audited at the campus. Depending on the documentation, IRS describes source code 20 as Erroneous Refunds or Regular Classification.

[43] GAO, *Internal Control: Standards for Internal Control in the Federal Government*, GAO/AIMD-00-21.3.1 (Washington, D.C.: November 1999).

[44] GAO, *Internal Control Management and Evaluation Tool*, GAO-01-1008G (Washington, D.C.: August 2001).

INDEX

S

T

W